D1566364

Self-Policing in Politics

THE POLITICAL ECONOMY OF REPUTATIONAL CONTROLS ON POLITICIANS

Glenn R. Parker

PRINCETON UNIVERSITY PRESS

PRINCETON AND OXFORD

Copyright © 2004 by Princeton University Press
Published by Princeton University Press, 41 William Street, Princeton,
New Jersey 08540
In the United Kingdom: Princeton University Press, 3 Market Place,
Woodstock, Oxfordshire OX20 1SY

LIBRARY OF CONGRESS CATALOGING-IN-PUBLICATION DATA

Parker, Glenn R., 1946–
Self-policing in politics: the political economy of reputational controls on politicians /
Glenn R. Parker.
p. cm.
Includes bibliographical references and index.
ISBN 0-691-11739-X
1. Political ethics—Economic aspects.   2. Political corruption—Economic aspects.
3. Self-control—Economic aspects.   4. Legislators—United States.   I. Title.
JA79.P353 2004
172′2—dc21   2003053640

British Library Cataloging-in-Publication Data is available

This book has been composed in Sabon

Printed on acid-free paper. ∞

www.pupress.princeton.edu

Printed in the United States of America

10 9 8 7 6 5 4 3 2 1

To Rocky, indomitable

Contents

List of Figures and Tables

Acknowledgments

I WOULD LIKE to acknowledge the assistance and support of several colleagues who have been instrumental in bringing this book to fruition. Over the years I have bombarded W. Mark Crain with questions about economic perspectives on opportunism in politics; likewise, I have peppered Morris Fiorina with questions about the value of reelection and the monopoly-like behavior of legislators. And, I could not have ever attempted to tackle the question of ethical behavior in politics had I not been able to spend my sabbatical at the Center for Study of Public Choice at George Mason University where I was first introduced to the study of public choice and, as some of my colleagues contend, the "dark side of politics." Chuck Myers, editor at Princeton University Press, did far more than merely shepherd my book through the evaluation process. His confidence in the manuscript, and his encouragement and support throughout the process, were of enormous value. I would be remiss if I did not mention the support of Suzie Parker, who was a receptive if not critical audience; we nonetheless remain husband and wife as well as good friends. Finally, my greatest debt is owed to the three reviewers who offered thoughtful insights and suggestions: Richard Fenno, Robert Tollison, and Michael Munger. I have tried to implement all of their suggestions and address their reservations. If I have failed in any respects, it is not for lack of effort. Nevertheless, I must bear the blame for any errors; these three scholars, however, share whatever success this book achieves.

Introduction

LIKE THE WISTFUL pursuit of the "philosopher's stone," in other words an imaginary substance believed capable of changing base metals into gold or silver, democratic theorists have long searched for mechanisms to control their politicians. Citizens' efforts to tar-and-feather their corrupt politicians have thankfully disappeared from politics altogether, largely replaced with an unfaltering belief that scandalous acts will be uncovered and the rascals subsequently thrown out of office. Both suppositions are debatable, however. Public choice theorists have called attention to the rational ignorance of voters that makes monitoring politicians extremely costly, perhaps prohibitively so; hence, learning of the wrongdoings of politicians is problematic at best. As for turning the rascals out of office, elections have proved rather ineffective in pruning governmental institutions of their corrupt members. For a variety of reasons, voters seem reluctant to replace public officials tainted by political scandal!

If elections and voter monitoring are chancy means for controlling politicians, citizens would seem to be at the mercy of their public officials. Perhaps so, but this does not mean that politicians, even rational ones, will necessarily exploit this situation; constraints on the ethical behavior of public officials could be self-imposed. This is not just wishful thinking. Individuals, especially rational ones, can be expected to behave ethically if they are adequately rewarded for doing so. For politicians, one reward for ethical conduct is a sterling reputation, which, beyond its intrinsic worth, serves at the same time as an electoral resource and a potentially attractive employee attribute if the politician should leave office voluntarily or involuntarily. Simply put, reputations can be viewed as representing investments by politicians that yield premiums in terms of electoral safety and post-elective employment. Reputations for honesty and ethical conduct don't come cheaply: Ethical conduct creates costs for rational politicians in terms of foregoing opportunities to avail themselves of the off-budget benefits of public office that are difficult to monitor. Rational politicians are unethical, therefore, because the benefits far exceed the potential or the expected costs of doing otherwise. One obvious cost (or loss) associated with dishonesty is the decline in reputability; or, put differently, unethical conduct drains the reputational goodwill that politicians have accumulated during their careers. Theoretically, a damaged reputation not only hurts politicians at election time but also when major private sector employers are considering hiring top-level executives.

Despite the relevance of reputations as mechanisms for inducing self-imposed constraints on unethical and dishonest behavior, political scientists have devoted little attention to this instrument of self-policing.[1] Economists have taken the lead on this question, no doubt because of their interest in the practices of businesses and the uncertainty that underlies many consumer purchases. Political scientists appear to ignore the striking similarities between the problems of opportunism facing voters and consumers. For instance, businesses skimp on the quality of materials, and politicians benefit their friends and relatives at the expense of voters. Indeed, there are strong parallels between the behaviors of businesses in the market, and politicians in office, in the sense that both encounter similar conditions facilitating cheating (e.g., consumer and voter ignorance, costs of monitoring).

Problems of cheating cover a wide range of economic and political behavior. Problems of "shirking," for example, arise among managers who pursue their own private interests rather than those of stockholders (Jensen and Meckling 1976), and among legislators who vote their own ideological preferences rather than those of their constituents (Kalt and Zupan 1984). The costs of monitoring enable managers to exercise discretion (Alchian and Demsetz 1972), and bureaucrats to escape detection for doing the same (Niskanan 1971). Businesses engage in post-contractual reneging (Klein et al. 1978), as do legislators (Weingast and Marshall 1988). Businesses "cheat" on quality by selling a low-quality product at the price reserved for high-quality products (Klein and Leffler 1981). Politicians "cheat" voters by pursuing their own private interests rather than giving a faithful effort to advancing the interests of their constituents (Kau and Rubin 1979).

Consequently, a particularly common (and troublesome) issue in both economic and political markets is one of assuring honesty and restraining opportunism (see, for example, Becker and Stigler 1974; Barro 1973; Ferejohn 1986; Akerlof 1970; Lott 1990; Fama and Jensen 1983; Shepsle and Weingast 1987; Telser 1980; Alchian and Demsetz 1972; Crain et al. 1986; Parker and Parker 1998a; Williamson 1975; Williamson 1981). This is the question addressed by this inquiry: the design of ex ante protections against the opportunistic behavior of politicians. Simply put, how can we assure that politicians behave faithfully, dedicated to their legislative responsibilities, eschewing unethical gain, and warranting the trust of their constituents? The similarity between this question and one frequently addressed by economists — namely, assuring that producers supply high-quality products despite consumer ignorance — encourages us to consider economic treatments of this problem. In this study, I explore a potential mechanism of *ethical control* that economists claim is effective in keeping businesses honest and reluctant about exploiting consumer ignorance to "cheat" in the production of high-quality goods: reputations or brand names. The paucity of empirical research on the effects of reputations on producer honesty and opportunism, as well as its uncertain implications for politics, makes this inquiry a worthwhile endeavor.

The substantive focus of this study is on the U.S. Congress and the behavior of its members. Economic treatments of Congress frequently focus on issues of representation and view the legislator–voter relationship as a principal–agent dilemma. That is, the "principal" employs an "agent" to act in the principal's best interests; but if all parties (principal and agent) are self-interested, then the "agent" may on occasion act in his or her own self-interest rather than that of the principal's. The dilemma is how to prevent legislator-agents from ignoring constituent opinion. "Constituent opinion" is often narrowly construed in economic as well as political analyses — that is, the issue preferences and opinions of voters. Hence, the research question is often approached in terms of the extent to which the roll-call votes of legislators match the opinions of their constituents. Although a very useful and important conceptualization, this is an unfortunately narrow construction of the demands of voters. Voters may ultimately accept less, but they desire politicians who are ostensibly bound to ethical codes of conduct. Legislators don't merely violate the agent–principal relationship when they express their own opinions rather than voting constituent sentiment. They also violate this relationship when they exploit their positions for private gain, since voters rarely prefer effective dishonest politicians to effective honest ones. (At the very least, the "take" of dishonest politicians reduces the budget surplus available to voters, such as tax cuts, and therefore should meet with constituent disapproval.) If our politicians were not merely self-interested, but also unethical, problems of representation would be compounded. Thus, the major questions of representation should be phrased: how do we assure that agents reflect constituent sentiment *and* forego the gains that can be obtained by exploiting public office? The latter question — assuring ethical behavior — is the focus of this inquiry.

PROBLEMS IN CONTROLLING LEGISLATORS

In the U.S. Congress, the behavior of legislators is regulated largely through ethical codes of conduct. Legislators are expected to behave within the confines of such ethical codes but if they do not, they are then subject to punishment and perhaps expulsion. In this way, ethics laws and codes are expected not merely to rid institutions of their most corrupt members, but also to deter others from following the same (corrupt) path. Unfortunately, ethics codes, like many other explicit forms of control, are subject to perverse problems of rational behavior on the part of legislators. Rational legislators could draft codes in such a way as to make them ineffective, either by including "loopholes," making information "confidential," "watering down" the codes, or limiting the range of transgressions and punishments. And if Congress were to become populated with a significant number of individuals interested in financial gain, we might expect them to fashion ethics codes that were quite lenient and filled with exemptions. A case in point is the legislative amendment to the 1971 Federal Election Campaign Act (passed in 1978) that prevented the allocation of campaign funds for personal use, but exempted legislators elected to the Ninety-sixth Congress from the provision! In sum, formal ethics codes only assure minimum standards which are implicitly only the *maximum enforceable*.

At first glance, monitoring seems a perfect means of controlling politicians and alleviating some of the problems involved in ethics codes. If monitoring is defined to include the investigation and disclosure of information about the activities of politicians, such information could highlight malfeasance and misdeeds. Even if the costs of monitoring were not prohibitive, there remains a major problem since the actions of politicians can be cleverly hidden from public view. Politicians possess information about their performance in office that is not available to their constituents, so the latter are in a poor position to judge that performance. Voters need this knowledge to make informed assessments but politicians have few incentives to provide it. There is no reason to believe that rational politicians will reveal information about their activities that might place their careers in jeopardy. Such asymmetries in information create moral-hazard problems: hidden actions.

Even more perverse, increased monitoring might just have the opposite effect — rather than diminishing cheating on the part of politicians, it may actually increase it. Where personalized relationships exist between principals and agents, any bilateral implicit contract incorporating aspects of trust could be impaired by increased monitoring. What results is more, rather than less, shirking:

> [T]he agent may perceive more intensive monitoring by the principal as an indication of distrust, or as a unilateral break of the contract built on mutual trust. As a consequence, the agent affected sees no reason why he or she should not behave in an opportunistic way. . . . [I]ncreased monitoring raises the marginal utility from shirking as the

agent's "bad conscience" is absolved by the breakdown of trust with the principal: Thus to some extent monitoring "crowds out" work effort. (Frey 1993, 664–665)

Moreover, since many of the activities assigned to politicians are difficult to define precisely, and there exist the aforementioned asymmetries in information that favor politicians, punishing politicians for failures in performance is likely to be difficult, if not futile, irrespective of monitoring.

Perhaps, punishment at the hands of voters is the ultimate deterrent to agent misbehavior. Unfortunately, in the last period — that is, the last term prior to exiting office — electoral reprisal will no longer serve as a significant threat. Elections may also fall prey to problems of adverse selection since they provide no assurance that the candidate pool will contain good alternatives to opportunistic incumbent legislators (Parker 1996). I will have more to say about the effectiveness of elections in eliminating dishonest and opportunistic legislators, and deterring unethical behavior, in chapter 6.

Ethics codes, monitoring, and elections simply cannot do the job of constraining cheating on the part of politicians. This does not mean that these mechanisms are totally ineffective in discouraging opportunistic behavior; rather, my contention is that we are far too dependent upon these "institutions" to deter unethical or quasi-ethical behavior. These instruments of control, at the very least, need to be supplemented by other mechanisms that are less likely to fall prey to perverse problems of rational behavior. One mechanism capable of serving this function is a politician's reputation. For the purpose of this study, reputations are conceptually defined as *publicly held conceptions of politicians' qualities*; in the marketplace, reputations serve a similar function — expectations of quality from the perspective of consumers (Miller and Plott 1985; Shapiro 1983, 663).

THE VALUE OF REPUTATIONS

There are numerous "signals" that firms transmit, aside from their reputations, to demonstrate the quality of their products — warranties, firm-specific signs, logos, price, advertising, and the like. For instance, high prices are thought to reflect a price premium that incorporates the costs to businesses of producing a high-quality product, as well as a normal rate of return to the firm for its reluctance to exploit consumer ignorance to produce low-quality goods — in other words, extortion money. The rationale is that businesses won't produce low-quality goods because of the fear of losing the enhanced returns (i.e., price premium).

From this perspective, market prices above the competitive level signal consumers that a firm is unlikely to cheat on quality. This lends support to the common adage: "You get what you pay for." Similarly, advertising (e.g., free samples) represents a nonsalvageable asset which signals consumers that the firm expects to recoup the costs of advertising from the flow of future business, which results from the production of quality goods.

From the perspective of voters and consumers, only signals of product quality that are bonded — some asset or wealth is forfeited if cheating is discovered — serve as effective signals of product quality (Ippolito 1990). The conceptualization of reputation used in this study meets this criterion: *A politician's reputation is bonded in the sense that career investments are lost if unethical behavior is uncovered.* In the marketplace, "the advertising of the name brand product indicates the presence of a current and future price premium. This premium on future sales is the firm's brand name capital which will be lost if the firm supplies lower than anticipated quality" (Klein and Leffler 1981, 632).

Models of the firm are relied upon in this analysis as conceptual and heuristic devices for yielding insights into the nature of reputations and their effects on politics. While there are many ways in which the study of the firm can better inform us about reputations, several conclusions drawn from this literature seem particularly relevant to the present inquiry. First, reputations serve as low-cost signals of product quality for consumers unaware of such matters prepurchase (i.e., prior to purchasing and using the product). In this way they short-cut the "search" costs incurred by consumers. Second, reputations are shaped by the "extended dealings" of businesses (i.e., consumers' experiences with a particular firm are shared with other potential buyers) that result in the pooling of information among consumers. Third, reputations represent investments in nonsalvageable capital that can deter cheating on the quality of a product, such as selling a low-quality product at a high-quality price because consumers lack the necessary prepurchase information. Fourth, reputations provide firms with a future earnings stream that is greater than the one-time gain from cheating and includes a "premium" to induce honesty. Finally, reputational controls can fall prey to last-period problems: the absence of future dealings encourages rational actors to ignore the returns from reputability and cheat prior to the cessation of present business arrangements. These propositions are incorporated into the analysis to explain how reputability promotes ethical conduct in politics, and the forces that threaten its effectiveness in this regard.

The significance of this study can be stated in a single, if not complex, sentence: To examine whether reputations for faithful and trustworthy behavior are capable of creating ex ante incentives for ethical conduct by rational politicians who possess hidden information; who are aware that the costs associated with monitoring their unethical behavior, as well as punishing it, are quite high, perhaps prohibitively so because of moral hazards; and who encounter a rationally ignorant electorate. All too frequently, as will be argued in later chapters, we have relied upon elections and ethics codes to ensure proper conduct on the part of public officials. Our faith in these two mechanisms clearly exceeds the capacity of either to effectively constrain unethical conduct. It seems that rational politicians can always find a loophole in an ethics code that will exonerate or justify their misfeasance, or a way to win election despite involvement in a scandal.

Ethics codes and elections also suffer from the fact that both are ex post mechanisms for the enforcement of ethical behavior — that is, punishment occurs after the unethical behavior has occurred. Moreover, the effectiveness of ethics codes and elections in this regard — topics addressed in later chapters — is suspect. Politicians involved in scandals seem to return to office in alarming numbers (chapter 6), and despite ethics reforms during the past half-century, political scandals continue to surface (chapter 1). This is not to imply that elections and ethics codes are irrelevant to controlling the ethical conduct of politicians; such a statement would be an exaggeration. But it is not an exaggeration to claim that these mechanisms of ethical enforcement need to be supplemented if we are serious about effectively controlling the behavior of our politicians. The establishment of a reputation as a faithful agent (i.e., honest, loyal, conscientious) may provide just such a mechanism to complement elections and ethics codes in encouraging ethical behavior among rational politicians.

As mentioned earlier, "brand names" cannot replace ethics codes and elections as deterrents to opportunistic or unethical behavior, but they are able to mitigate some of the problems that seem to plague these explicit mechanisms of legislator control. For instance, reputations enable voters to differentiate among candidates and to distinguish the honest from the dishonest, the trustworthy from the untrustworthy. Ethics codes establish only minimum standards of conduct, but reputations may result in *implicit* contractual adherence that even exceeds levels established by ethics codes. Ethics codes are possibly a necessary, but certainly not a sufficient, condition for deterring opportunism. In conjunction with reputations, ethics codes gain vitality. Obedience to ethics codes enhances one's reputation for trustworthiness: politicians trumpet their adherence to ethics codes, or their absence from ethics investigations, as evidence of their trustworthiness.

If politicians seek to protect their reputations, they have incentives to avoid activities that would tarnish their brand names. In economics, tarnishing one's reputation is equivalent to destroying previously invested capital, the irrationality of which limits the rationality of opportunism. Thus, reputable politicians avoid engaging in opportunism because they fear the loss of investments in their political careers, and the premiums those investments earn. This creates a form of self-policing.

Some economists contend that a major difference between the brand names of firms and politicians is that firms are able to "sell" their brand names while politicians cannot.

> Past investments by politicians in advertising and good will (i.e., brand name) invariably assist them in producing support in the present. Yet, unlike a firm, politicians have only very limited ways of selling this political human capital. For example, they can endorse another candidate, but cannot sell the new candidate his name or his office. Politicians receive quasi-rents from these past investments, but are unable to fully sell the rights to this rental stream to others. (Lott 1986, 88)

Thus, incentives for reputability are possibly greater in economic than political markets. Perhaps, but we should not exaggerate this distinction since politicians may be able to cash in on their reputability in post-elective employment. For instance, if reputability influences the post-elective earning opportunities of politicians, then the better one's reputation, the better are those employment opportunities. Under these circumstances, reputations are *unlikely* to be "milked," even in the last period of officeholding. Economists have gained an appreciation of this mechanism for controlling opportunism in business dealings: "If one party's reputation for nonopportunistic dealings can be sold and used in later transactions in an infinite-time-horizon economy, the firm that cheats in the 'last' period to any one buyer from the firm experiences a capital loss" (Klein et al. 1978, 304). This is a major premise of the analysis.

REPUTATIONAL CONTROLS

As political scientists, we have a relatively elementary understanding of how reputations function to keep our politicians honest. All too frequently, we characterize "bad reputations" as merely damaging politicians' prospects for reelection. But, of course, there is considerable evidence to the contrary (see chapter 6). So how do reputations function to constrain cheating by politicians? Economists provide some clues about the features of reputations that promote nonopportunistic behavior. In order to better understand the role of reputations in constraining unethical behavior in politics, I fashion a model of reputational control drawn from propositions in the economic study of the firm. This model describes several incentives associated with reputability that encourage ethical behavior, and suggests some empirical hypotheses for testing. The model is based upon five propositions that I term assumptions about reputational control. They describe various properties of reputations that encourage honesty in the market.

A basic premise commonly used in economic inquiry is that *individuals are rational and utility-maximizing*. The same proposition is employed in this study to account for the behavior of politicians and voters. As rational individuals, we expect voters to value (and seek) shortcuts to becoming informed and predicting the behavior of their representatives (e.g., evaluating political information and politicians). Reputations serve this purpose by *reducing the search costs incurred by voters*. This is the second assumption. Since voters desire simple cues for evaluating and predicting political behavior, politicians develop them. Reputations are linked to the behavior of politicians because the latter have incentives to create consistency between their reputations and behavior: Reputations won't be useful to voters unless they are backed up with behavior; otherwise, reputations are merely statements and not reliable predictors of behavior — "cheap talk." Voters aren't interested in statements or words, only actions, and unless some evidence can be mustered to demonstrate that a reputation is related to behavior, reputations are useless. In this sense, reputations must be validated through behavior. Validating one's reputation to the satisfaction of voters requires politicians to make investments (i.e., sunk costs) by engaging in certain expected behaviors. Doing so entails costs to politicians by requiring them to forego other opportunities and behaviors (i.e., opportunity costs).

Reputations are also spread through networks of individuals (e.g., consumers, voters) who have had personal dealings with an economic actor (e.g., firm) or agent. People who have had contacts or dealings with an agent can spread the word to others about their experiences and the latter's performance. Of course there are other avenues available for obtaining reputational information about politicians, such as reports from good government groups, newspapers, and the like, but the costs of making use of these mechanisms are often far greater than free-riding on the experiences of others to obtain this information. Consumers frequently rely upon information gathered by others, in lieu of the claims made through advertising, when making market decisions involving the quality of products that cannot be determined pre-purchase — conditions ripe for cheating on product quality. This is the third assumption. Fourth, *reputations represent sunk investments*. As economic agents form reputations, they incur costs in the effort, such as the establishment of consumer services. Reputations incorporate the past decisions and costs incurred by economic agents in nurturing consumer loyalty and appeal.

The above propositions are as relevant to politics as they are to economics. Voters and politicians are always seeking to maximize their returns, and both gain from methods that shortcut the costs involved in obtaining information. Reputations in politics are also spread through networks of individuals who have had personal experiences with a politician, or his or her office. Voters share their experiences with others, and for many voters, this is the only information that reaches their ears. And politicians, like commercial businesses, also make investments in their reputations, investments that might be lost if they were discovered as engaging in actions contrary to the desires of their customers — voters. This should make politicians reticent about damaging their reputations and sacrificing their accumulated career investments by engaging in unethical behavior.

The fifth proposition has its roots in the study of the brand names of businesses, but it is modified here so that it is more applicable to the study of politicians' reputations. Reputations are designed to ensure a continuous stream of customers — repeat purchases by past and present customers, and purchases from first-time and future buyers who, unaware of the quality of a product, base their decisions on brand names. This long-term profit stream, containing a "price premium" to ensure both quality and honesty, is one of the major benefits derived from reputations under competitive market conditions. Nonetheless, describing the reputations of politicians in this vein seems rather strange. Rather than ensuring a stream of customers, I assume that *reputations yield job security for politicians.* The similarity between the economic interpretation of reputations and that advanced here is that both conceptualizations envision reputations as ensuring a future earnings stream containing a price premium. The premium honest businesses obtain is a higher price, over-and-above average variable costs. For politicians, the premium is paid in terms of electoral safety, and prestigious job opportunities if they leave their present position voluntarily or involuntarily. Reputations function in the same way for politicians as for businesses since they both enhance the prospects of future gain.

Implicit in the last assumption is the notion that politicians, like all employees, value job security. Does this by itself negate unethical conduct? While economic entrepreneurs may trade job security for handsome, more risky returns, the former remains a goal of every rational economic agent. But just because politicians, like employees, want to keep their jobs does not mean that either is totally risk averse. Clearly,

the existence of legislator opportunism and managerial shirking is sufficient to demonstrate that both are willing to take a chance now and
then to obtain private gain, acutely aware that their actions might
threaten job security if uncovered.

Job security is not merely defined here in terms of reelection, as it is
in most studies; rather, it also includes employment opportunities that
incumbent legislators could obtain should their political careers come to
an end. This is not to dismiss the force of reelection as a potent factor
motivating the behavior of legislators (see, for instance, Fiorina 1977,
and Mayhew 1974). But job security entails more than just reelection.
Legislators want assurances that should they ever leave Congress they
can obtain attractive post-elective employment (i.e., prestigious jobs).
That is, legislators "demand" assurances not merely that they will find a
job, but that the job will be a *really good one*. This is the *premium*
awarded trustworthy, dutiful politicians.

These last three propositions — consumer intercommunication of experiences, job security, and sunk investments — describe the major market (economic) incentives associated with reputations that constrain
cheating in both economic and political markets. Politicians fear damage to their reputations, if word should spread from voter to voter
about their opportunism in office; businesses fear that information sharing by dissatisfied customers will hurt their brand names. For politicians, tarnished reputations can engender reelection defeat and few attractive post-elective employment opportunities. Businesses suffer in a
similar manner when their brand names are blemished, as future sales
are lost as well as any premiums they receive above the market price for
their products. Finally, if revelations of the wrongdoings of politicians
or businesses become public, both lose some of the capital invested in
their reputations. In politics, such capital includes not only the time and
effort required in building a career in politics, or gaining political office,
but also the entrepreneurial activity that is required in establishing political vocations. In business, reputations represent nonsalvageable assets; hence, time and money spent in creating an appealing reputation
are lost if cheating is discovered. Moreover, these three reputational incentives, or controls, are interconnected, which compounds the effects
of each. For instance, if consumers (voters) spread word of a firm's
(politician's) cheating, the firm (politician) loses reputational capital,
any price premium it is presently earning, and future sales. And losses
of reputational capital threaten future earnings, sales, price premiums,
and so on. A major objective of this study is to see how well these
conditions or incentives for reputational control in economic markets
apply to the behavior of legislators.

Objectives

The present study represents the evolution in my thinking about the control of public officials. This interest was first sparked by my study of the uncanny efforts by legislators to expand their discretion—that is, their ability to do whatever they wanted (Parker 1992). These results prompted another research question: how would a discretion-maximizing legislature operate in an environment where rent seeking (attempts to obtain economic advantage through the political process) had become an established mode for doing business (Parker 1996)? The inquiry into this latter question reached the conclusion that the nature of the rent-seeking society seemed to be producing over-time changes in the composition of Congress. Specifically, Congress was becoming more hospitable to individuals seeking material gain (extrinsic rewards) and less attractive to those interested in the intrinsic gains derived from public service, such as power, recognition, and national visibility. The resulting "adverse selection" of candidates for public office ostensibly weakens the effectiveness of elections as a means for reprimanding rent-seeking legislators since the candidate pool evolves so that it is largely comprised of the latter type of individuals. With little to choose from, voters confront the choice of selecting among "evils." But even if elections were effective in punishing politicians for their wrongdoings, they represent ex post mechanisms of control and are ineffective in the last period of officeholding. What is needed is a mechanism to complement electoral sanctions that functions ex ante.

The major question prompting this inquiry is to what extent reputability might serve as a mechanism to constrain unethical conduct in Congress, and what conditions might enhance, or limit, its capacity to do so. Or more grossly, do reputations keep politicians honest? There is also a tangential objective to this study. The inquiry is designed to introduce political scientists to economic reasoning about reputations, and how such thinking about reputations can be usefully incorporated into the study of politics and politicians.

Conclusion

It goes without saying that a "good" reputation is rewarding in-and-of-itself. Reputability, however, also earns material benefits that compound its value in politics and markets. The behavior of the "firm" serves as a heuristic device in identifying these additional rewards to reputability because, from the perspective of the firm, only material (economic) benefits matter. Thus, by focusing on the economic payoffs from "brand names," we can identify the features of reputations that are materially beneficial. This book is about how such material rewards operate in politics, and whether they alone are sufficient to deter opportunism.

Models of the firm suggest that reputable businesses are deterred from cheating their customers for at least three reasons: waste of sunk costs (capital), loss of a price premium, and fear of consumer boycott. Likewise, politicians can be expected to avoid cheating or engaging in unethical activity because they fear the loss of: (1) sunk investments they have made in their careers in politics; (2) premiums paid to ethical politicians in terms of electoral security and post-elective employment; and/or (3) future voter support, as constituents spread word of past experiences with politicians. Simply put, reputations operate to deter opportunism in business and politics by creating incentives for ethical and nonopportunistic dealings. These do not, of course, describe the myriad of ways that reputations operate to induce nonopportunistic behavior, but these three provide a good start in studying reputational controls in politics since they are mentioned frequently in the economic literature.

As noted earlier, the study of reputations or brand names by economists has far surpassed the efforts of political scientists; however, many economic treatments of the topic have been highly theoretical and mathematical. While these analyses are useful in advancing our understanding of the properties of reputations, with relatively few exceptions, the propositions derived from them have rarely been applied to politicians, or subject to extensive empirical testing. Therefore, the present inquiry hopes to contribute to our understanding of reputations by strengthening the empirical bases for existing economic theories and propositions about reputations. In addition, this study offers a rather unique solution to the last-period problem in politics that builds upon important economic ideas and insights. I hope economists will find these aspects of the book appealing, as well as the parallels between the firm and the behavior of politicians. For political scientists, I hope this inquiry will enhance the relevance of reputations, and how economic theories can provide insights into the ways in which reputations operate in politics.

In chapter 1 I introduce the issue of opportunism and describe economic and political solutions to this problem. Chapter 2 elaborates on why reputations control cheating in economics and politics. The objective of chapter 3 is to describe problems in the market for legislators — biased information, difficulties in legislator monitoring, and conditions that erode the premiums awarded ethical politicians — that mitigate the effectiveness of reputational controls on unethical conduct. The methodology underlying the analysis is described in chapter 4. The major question prompting this inquiry—can reputational capital deter opportunism in legislatures—is explored in chapter 5. Chapter 6 is devoted to examining the extent to which trustworthiness is rewarded with electoral safety and prestigious post-elective employment. In chapter 7, weaknesses in reputational controls are examined. Among the questions addressed in this chapter is whether first-hand contact with legislators creates a sufficiently critical audience for ensuring the latter's ethical conduct. The concluding chapter summarizes the themes and arguments made throughout the book, and discusses some of the implications that can be drawn from this inquiry.

CHAPTER 1

What Is Opportunism and How Do We Control It?

IT WOULD BE NICE (but naive) to believe that *opportunism — that is, devious conduct of an unethical or quasi-ethical nature —* is purely seasonal or restricted to distinct periods of time (for example, elections), confined to certain activities (for example, foreign travel), or only exhibited by a single branch of government (for example, the House of Representatives). Then we could theoretically isolate acts of opportunism under these conditions, and fashion explicit mechanisms of monitoring to uncover and punish these transgressions. Unfortunately, this is not the case. No institution is spared, and few activities are entirely immune from exploitation.

My remarks should not be read to imply that all politicians who engage in acts of opportunism are ostensibly corrupt. In the first place, acts of opportunism are usually *not* overtly illegal; they represent unethical or quasi-ethical expressions of deception and deceit — lapses in character. Second, most acts of opportunism rarely blossom into full-blown legislative investigations, possibly because legislators are not eager to investigate practices that many have indulged in at one time or another. Finally, acts of opportunism rarely receive the public notoriety that explicit displays of corruption receive, perhaps because the economic gain is far less in the former than the latter. For instance, retiring legislators who travel unnecessarily at public expense in their final term — lame-duck junkets — are certainly acting opportunistically, but they cannot obtain financial returns anything close to what legislators obtained through explicit bribes in the Abscam scandal. Nonetheless, given voter ignorance, and the costs of monitoring, acts of opportunism may occur with greater frequency than acts of outright corruption, and leave an equally indelible stain on our political institutions.

We can characterize opportunism as representing a lack of candor or honesty on the part of public officials. Deception is a distinguishing feature of opportunism. Such a description mirrors the use of the concept in economics:

> The assumption that individuals behave in a self-interested way is so commonplace to economics that it would seem scarcely to warrant separate attention. Opportunism, however, is more than simple self-

> interest seeking. It is self-interest seeking with guile: agents who are
> skilled at dissembling realize transactional advantages. Economic
> man, assessed with respect to his transactional characteristics, is thus
> a more subtle and devious creature than the usual self-interest as-
> sumption reveals. Opportunism can involve either data distortion or
> the making of self-disbelieved promises. (Williamson 1975, 255)

Opportunism may seem innocent enough to ignore because the focus is
less on corruption in the illegal sense and more on the devious unethical
or quasi-ethical behavior of economic or political agents. Although acts
of opportunism are not normally illegal, frequently represent minor personal gain, and taken individually amount to little relative to the government budget, the accumulation of these small acts of self-interest are
important because they destroy citizen faith in the political system. "Political legitimacy is undermined if government permits some to obtain
disproportionate private gains at the expense of others" (Rose-Ackerman 1999, 226). This would seem to be especially troublesome if those
obtaining the gain are public officials. In addition, a plausible argument
could be made that opportunism is a gateway to higher levels of corruption.[1] Kiting checks and exploiting loopholes in campaign finance laws,
for example, may be just a few short steps away from trading favors for
bribes. Academic arguments notwithstanding, do voters really care about
such expressions of devious self-interest?

IS OPPORTUNISM SOMETHING TO WORRY ABOUT?

It takes little to convince people that corruption is a problem that war-
rants concern and remedy. For this reason, most attention has been
given to explicit acts of corruption, such as bribery. Still, opportunism is
far more ubiquitous, equally damaging to the political system, and perhaps more difficult to police due to moral hazards.[2] If opportunistic
actions normally result in little monetary gain, and are costly to police,
do voters really care about politicians engaging in opportunism? Are
legislators convinced that there is a pressing need to restrict and monitor potential areas of opportunism? The answer seems to be in the affir-
mative for both statements. For instance, there seems little doubt that
constituents are wary of the foreign travel of House incumbents: They
harbor deep suspicions that foreign travel is a mere disguise for a paid
vacation (table 1.1)! For instance, 86 percent of those interviewed in a
national survey in 1977 expressed little worry over trips that entailed
work, but 76 percent agreed with the statement that "too often when
congressmen go abroad, they are wined and dined and taken in by the
leaders they talk with." And House incumbents tended to agree with

TABLE 1.1
Public Attitudes Toward Congressional Foreign Travel

Statement	N	Agree (%)	Disagree (%)	Not Sure (%)
"The trouble with many trips congressmen take is that they go off on junkets to have a good time and not to do serious business."	1532	73	14	13
"There should be much tougher controls on just how essential a trip taken by a congressman is to his understanding more about a situation or program he is looking into."	1535	91	4	6
"Too often when congressmen go abroad, they are wined and dined and taken in by the leaders they talk with."	1535	76	10	13
"I'm not so much concerned with the number of trips a congressman takes abroad so long as they are working trips and not just disguised vacations."	1534	86	10	5

Source: U.S. House of Representatives, *Final Report of the Commission on Administrative Review* (1977, 841–842).

their constituents: 60 percent favored prohibiting lame-duck travel, and another 25 percent favored restrictions; only 14 percent favored no changes whatsoever (table 1.2).

The same level of agreement is evident when consideration is given to honoraria, another potential area for opportunism: both House incumbents and the broader mass public are concerned about the acceptance of honoraria (table 1.3). Occasional speeches, whether given to an interest group or academic audience, bother few incumbents or constituents, but the picture changes dramatically when attention shifts to speeches that are financially lucrative, either because the speeches are numerous or the speaking fees are large. For example, while less than 30 percent of either the sample of the public, or the sample of House incumbents, are concerned about a legislator making an occasional speech to a university audience for a small fee, 71 percent of the mass public and 89 percent of the House incumbents worry about a member of Congress making a *number* of speeches to an interest group for which he or she

TABLE 1.2
Attitudes of House Incumbents toward Lame-Duck Travel[a]

Attitude	Percent
Leave it alone	14
Restrict but do not prohibit	25
Prohibit	60
Not sure	1
N =	146

Source: U.S. House of Representatives, *Final Report of the Commission on Administrative Review* (1977, 920).

[a]*Question:* "How do you feel the House ought to deal with the question of foreign travel by lame-duck Members—do you feel that this is something which ought to be left alone and that no further rules are required, do you believe that foreign travel by lame ducks ought to be restricted in some fashion, or do you feel that foreign travel by lame ducks ought to be prohibited?"

receives large fees (table 1.3). Thus, there is agreement between the public and political elites as to what constitutes devious practices, and the misuse of one's position—taking honoraria and lame-duck travel—seems to qualify. These two areas of opportunism are examined in this analysis.

It is interesting to note that many of the voters who expressed concern about the taking of honoraria put a great deal of faith in the ability of elections to keep politicians honest and to curb abuse. Even in instances where a congressman gives "a number of speeches" and exacts "large fees," 57 percent of the public were satisfied with the situation if the voters knew about the behavior and could vote for (or against) that member at the next election (table 1.4). But note, House incumbents are less sanguine about the matter: only 30 percent of the House incumbents believed that public knowledge of these conditions would allay their concerns about honoraria (table 1.4). Clearly, voters put greater faith in elections as controls on politicians than politicians themselves seem to. Perhaps legislators are far more aware of the costs of monitoring public officials and the problems involved in defeating entrenched incumbents, and voters are far too naive.

This analysis examines several examples of opportunism or unethical behavior that could result in monetary gain (e.g., kiting checks), or merely trading work for leisure (e.g., lame-duck travel, voting absences). All of these actions share a common trait: they can be exploited in a devious, self-interested, and unethical or quasi-unethical manner. As noted earlier, problems of opportunism are not unique to politics. Economists have taken a particular interest in such issues and have identified

TABLE 1.3
Attitudes of Mass Public and House Incumbents toward Honoraria for Speeches

Situation	Mass Public				House Incumbents			
	N	Bothers Me (%)	Does Not Bother Me (%)	Not Sure (%)	N	Bothers Me (%)	Does Not Bother Me (%)	Not Sure (%)
A Congressman makes an occasional speech to a university or academic audience for which he receives a small fee.	1,524	29	64	7	144	28	70	3
A Congressman makes an occasional speech to business, trade, labor, or environmental groups which are affected by his work in Congress for which he receives a small fee.	1,531	39	52	8	144	45	53	2
A Congressman makes a number of speeches to business, trade, labor, or environmental groups which are affected by his work in Congress for which he receives small fees.	1,530	50	41	9	144	57	41	2
A Congressman makes an occasional speech to business, trade, labor, or environmental groups which are affected by his work in Congress for which he receives large fees.	1,532	67	26	8	144	85	13	3
A Congressman makes a number of speeches to business, trade, environmental, or labor groups which are affected by his work in Congress and he receives a large fee for such speeches.	1,529	71	21	8	144	89	9	2

Source: U.S. House of Representatives, *Final Report of the Commission on Administrative Review* (1977, 845–846 and 910–911).

TABLE 1.4
Perceptions of Mass Public and House Incumbents toward the Effectiveness of Elections in Curtailing Honoraria[a]

Situation	Mass Public				House Incumbents			
	N	Concerns Satisfied (%)	Not Satisfied (%)	Not Sure (%)	N	Concerns Satisfied (%)	Not Satisfied (%)	Not Sure (%)
A Congressman makes an occasional speech to a university or academic audience for which he he receives a small fee.	427	67	29	5	40	64	34	3
A Congressman makes an occasional speech to business, trade, labor, or environmental groups which are affected by his work in Congress for which he receives a small fee.	596	67	29	5	64	67	32	2
A Congressman makes a number of speeches to business, trade, labor, or environmental groups which are affected by his work in Congress for which he receives small fees.	756	65	30	5	82	55	44	1
A Congressman makes an occasional speech to business, trade, labor, or environmental groups which are affected by his work in Congress for which he receives large fees.	1,010	59	36	5	119	38	61	13
A Congressman makes a number of speeches to business, trade, environmental or labor groups which are affected by his work in Congress and he receives a large fee for such speeches.	1,077	57	39	4	126	30	68	2

Source: U.S. House of Representatives, Final Report of the Commission on Administrative Review (1977, 845–846 and 910–911).
[a] Question: "Would your concerns about that situation be substantially satisfied or not if the voters in the Member's district were made fully aware of his or her situation and could vote for or against the Member at the next election?" Only asked of respondents "bothered" by action. Minor

several conditions that encourage opportunistic behavior on the part of rational economic actors. In the next several pages, I describe examples of opportunism in politics and economics so that the reader has a better understanding of how this behavior manifests itself.

OPPORTUNISM IN ECONOMICS

There are numerous examples of opportunism arising in economic behavior, but five of the most discussed are: adverse selection (hidden information), moral hazards (hidden actions), last-period exploitation, reneging (in contracts), and shirking. These problems plague economic transactions, resulting in inefficiencies and biases that disrupt market economics in the purest sense. In the following pages, I describe the nature of these problems, and how they promote opportunism in economic relationships.

Adverse selection arises when one party to a trade, for example the buyer, cannot recognize certain *relevant* characteristics, such as honesty, of the other party, for example the seller. Under these conditions, the former has no way of knowing whether he or she is being cheated in any transactions with the latter. Buyers clearly suffer from hidden information. In the market, although the seller knows the quality of the goods produced, consumers are frequently unable to detect the quality of those goods prepurchase. Such circumstances tend to result in the production of suboptimal levels of quality in goods (Akerlof 1970; Leland 1979) as well as politicians (Parker 1996). Furthermore, if the market for services or products has evolved so that the pool of sellers leaves buyers with little to choose from (for example, in terms of honesty), there is no assurance that competition will alleviate the problem. In fact, adverse selection may actually drive out legitimate, honest sellers from the market. Nobel Laureate George Akerlof (1970) has provided, arguably, the clearest statement of this problem in his classic article on the evolution of the used car market into a market for "lemons."

Akerlof characterizes the market for automobiles as being composed of four kinds of cars: new cars and used cars, good cars and "lemons" (i.e., mechanically troublesome). While a buyer has no way of knowing whether a new car is a good one or a lemon at the time of purchase, after a length of time, the owner can form a more accurate idea of the quality of the car. The owner of the car has now become a potential seller (of the car), and has more knowledge about the quality of the car than potential buyers. Since it is impossible for buyers to determine differences between a good or bad car—only the seller knows—good cars can command no higher price than bad cars. This provides incentives for owners of bad cars to trade them to used car dealers, while owners of good cars have equally strong incentives to hold on to a "good thing." After all, if the latter had to purchase a new car, they would still risk the possibility of getting a potential lemon. Thus, "lemons" are traded in, and good cars only rarely.

The "lemons problem" is not merely about the inevitable effects of asymmetries in available information; it is also relevant to discussions of dishonesty and opportunism. If goods in a market may be sold honestly or dishonestly—valid or invalid representations of product quality—the presence of individuals willing to offer inferior goods will drive the sellers of quality goods out of existence. Why? Because consumers will expect low-quality products and will not purchase goods above the minimum cost associated with lower quality products:

> There may be potential buyers of good quality products and there may be potential sellers of such products in the appropriate price range; however, the presence of people who wish to pawn bad wares as good wares tends to drive out the legitimate business. The cost of dishonesty, therefore, lies not only in the amount by which the purchaser is cheated; the cost must include the loss incurred from driving legitimate business out of existence. (Akerlof 1970, 495)

A closely related problem is the existence of moral hazards (hidden actions). A moral hazard arises whenever there are incentives for economic agents, who cannot be easily monitored, to behave in a manner contrary to what is expected of them. If, for example, the efforts of employees cannot be measured, how can a firm be sure that they put forth the expected amount of effort? In fact, if employees receive a fixed salary, and their efforts cannot be effectively monitored, they may be tempted to act opportunistically by accepting payment without carrying out the duties they are being paid to perform—in other words, trading work for leisure. The source of this moral-hazard problem is, as with adverse-selection problems, an asymmetry of information among individuals resulting from the fact that some individual actions cannot be observed and hence contracted upon. An example may help to clarify the nature of this problem.

Let us suppose that mechanical problems with cars fall into two categories: major or minor problems. The two types of problems necessitate different costs—a major problem costs considerably more to repair than a minor one. When a car owner takes his or her car in for repairs, an asymmetry in information unfolds. The car repair expert may be tempted to tell the car owner whose car is afflicted with a minor problem, that it requires major repairs, charge a large amount for the repair, and then simply fix the minor problem. Assuming the car runs properly after the repair, the car owner will be satisfied and will have no reason to question the repairs or their costs. Hence, the car repair expert has an incentive to deceive his or her customers in order to earn more money than is justified by the amount of work actually required to repair the automobile. A natural remedy to this as well as other moral-hazard problems is to invest resources in monitoring. While I will have more to say about this solution to problems of economic opportunism in the next section of this chapter, let it suffice at this point to note that although feasible in simple situations where complete monitoring is possible, full observation of actions in most situations involving moral hazards is either impossible or prohibitively costly.

Although not particularly pervasive in market behavior, last-period problems can arise when an economic producer decides to go out of business, and immediately before exiting the market, sells deficient goods or services. No longer needing to worry about future business and customers, the "notorious business" dupes its customers by selling low-quality goods or services at the price reserved for high-quality products. As long as businesses depend upon a flow of future customers and sales, competitive pressures will constrain misrepresentation and opportunistic behavior. Once the need for future sales disappears, so does the market incentive that makes opportunism so unprofitable.

Opportunism also creeps into economic relations as a result of the openness of contracts. Contracts are frequently viewed as a means for assuring that economic agents pursue the aims of their employers. Unfortunately, contracts are not so easily fashioned. For example, no matter how precise the language, contractual disagreements can arise that require judicial intervention. But the problems with contracts run deeper: problems of observability and incompleteness create transactions that are subject to ex post opportunism. For instance, imperfect observability — for example, difficulties encountered in separating an agent's contribution from random events, or when an agent has private information about the quality of a good being sold — creates problems similar to those associated with moral hazards and adverse selection. Imperfect observability permits agents "slack," thereby assuring them latitude in their transactions and performance. And, contracts are inevitably incomplete since it is virtually impossible to anticipate and plan for all contingencies — either the contingencies are too numerous, or too costly, to anticipate completely. This makes the enforcement of contracts problematic and costly in many instances.

Opportunism can also be found in economic situations where individuals cooperate and work together as a team to obtain gains that exceed their individual inputs. The output in these situations is yielded by a "team" and is not merely the sum of the separable contributions of each of its members. Under such conditions, it is very difficult to reward individuals on the basis of their specific contribution and marginal productivity. Since the output is yielded by a "team," and it is impossible or quite costly to measure marginal productivity and make payments to team members in accord therewith, incentives for team members to "shirk" — that is, to trade work for leisure — exist:

> If his relaxation cannot be detected perfectly at zero cost, part of its effects will be borne by others in the team, thus making *his* realized cost of relaxation less than the true total cost to the team. The difficulty of detecting such actions permits the private costs of his actions to be less than their full costs. Since each person responds to his private realizable rate of substitution (in production) rather than the true total (i.e., social) rate, and so long as there are costs for other people to detect his shift toward relaxation, it will not pay (them) to force him to readjust completely by making him realize the true cost. Only enough effort will be made to equate the marginal costs of detection; and that implies a lower rate of productive effort and more shirking than in a costless monitoring, or measuring, world. (Alchian and Demsetz 1972, 780)

Put more simply, the inability to separate the product of individual effort raises the cost of assessing the marginal productivities of input owners; hence, incentives are created for employees to "shirk." Moreover, because costs are incurred in monitoring each other, team members (or input owners) will have more incentive to shirk when they work as part of a team, than if their individual efforts could be easily monitored.

Opportunism in Politics

If opportunism is a direct outgrowth of ostensible self-interest, we can expect it to afflict political as well as economic behavior, since both are often guided by principles of rational self-interest. Bold expressions of devious self-interested (opportunistic) behavior, for example, can be seen in the quasi-ethical or unethical nature of several legislative activities examined in this study: congressional junketing immediately prior to leaving office (for example, as a result of retirement), shirking in legislative roll-call voting (i.e., lack of attendance), extracting "rents" from businesses and groups in need (or fear) of governmental action, and kiting checks at the House bank. In each instance, congressional privileges or prerogatives are exploited in a devious self-interested fashion, resulting in quasi-ethical or unethical behavior.

As noted earlier in this chapter, congressional junketing has been a sore point with many citizens. From the perspectives of voters, too many legislators exploit congressional responsibilities to travel abroad. Instead of gathering important information to aid in congressional deliberations, they vacation at government expense. Such junketing is especially a problem when legislators plan to leave office; then, the fear that overseas travel might anger voters, no matter how cleverly disguised or justified, would be insufficient to deter foreign junketing. Without fear of electoral reprisal for foreign junkets, opportunistic legislators might travel extensively. In this way, foreign junketing constitutes a potential last-period problem in politics.

In addition to last-period problems, both economic and political relationships are plagued by another problem: shirking. Politicians and voters are involved in a principal–agent relationship in which the former are expected to faithfully represent the political preferences of their constituents. The difficulties inherent in policing this relationship provide opportunities for legislator-agents to shirk — for example, express their own preferences rather than those of their constituents (ideological shirking). Shirking can also occur in a manner that more closely approximates the rational opportunistic behavior of employees in a team-production situation: supplying less than a faithful effort in the execution of one's duties. This form of shirking is evident in the participation of legislators in policy making — that is, the lack of attendance for congressional floor votes. In other words, legislators who miss votes (participatory shirking) can be viewed as acting opportunistically toward their responsibilities. Given the ease with which legislators can now cast their votes (i.e., electronic voting), and the extent to which the legislative schedule is responsive to the demands placed on legislators (e.g., the need to spend time back home), it is a wonder that any votes are missed at all; and, indeed, very few are missed. Nonetheless, the difficulty in monitoring floor attendance, the existence of moral hazards, and the myriad of explanations that can be employed to justify absences, assure adequate incentives for opportunistic legislators to miss floor votes (i.e., shirk).

Opportunism in economic relationships is often associated with pecuniary gain; so, too, in politics. Two examples of the opportunistic behavior of politicians resulting in monetary gain are the honoraria incomes collected by representatives and senators, and the check-kiting scandal at the House bank. Until recently, legislators received payments from groups and businesses for minor personal appearances such as giving brief speeches. These honoraria provided legislators with some direct cash, as well as a readily available tax-deductible "contribution." Often the payment was far greater than the effort or the opportunity cost of the activity—an insidious example of rent extractions by legislators (Parker 1996).

A second example of opportunistic behavior leading to financial advantage is the capacity of House members to "bounce" checks without having to pay a penalty for doing so. Until recently prohibited due to scandals and investigations, House incumbents could, in essence, float a loan without paying a fee or any interest. Enterprising, opportunistic legislators could write checks on overdrawn accounts without much fear that their checks would be returned to the recipients. They need not ever worry that returned checks would carry an embarrassing adjoining notification of insufficient funds on deposit to cover the check. Rarely were members forced to even cover their debts, though the House bank frequently notified the delinquent. Thus, by extracting payments from groups with an interest in government policy under the guise of honoraria, and kiting checks at the House bank—knowingly issuing checks on accounts deficient in funds—legislators engaged in opportunistic behavior that enabled them to capture monetary gains through the auspices of their positions.

To summarize, opportunism can be found in both economics and politics. In economics, opportunism can be seen in problems involving adverse selection, last-period situations, reneging, moral hazards, and shirking. On the political side, opportunism can be seen in foreign junketing, lax voting attendance, collecting honoraria income, and kiting checks at the House bank. If opportunism can be found in both economic and political transactions, means for constraining opportunism or mitigating its effects may entail economic as well as political solutions. The political problems described above (foreign junketing, missing roll-call votes, taking honoraria, and kiting checks) have primarily relied upon political solutions as remedies—namely, elections and ethics codes.

POLITICAL SOLUTIONS TO OPPORTUNISM: ETHICS CODES AND ELECTIONS

An unfortunate observation about American politics is that, for the most part, voters have been quite lenient toward scandalized politicians. For instance, more than two-thirds of those congressional candidates accused of corruption, and running in the general election, were re-elected to the next Congress (Peters and Welch 1980, 703; Welch and Hibbing 1997, 233). Moreover, elections operate to punish incumbents *after* they have committed acts of corruption. And if these defects or imperfections were not enough to weaken the electoral incentive for honesty, elections are rendered totally ineffective for legislators seeking retirement (voluntary) from office; needless to say, retirement from office is a major source of turnover in the membership of Congress. Granted, the threat of electoral defeat might operate as an ex ante instrument to constrain opportunism by influencing expectations, but only until a decision to retire has been made. If a legislator plans to exit, the threat evaporates and the constraint on opportunism likewise disappears. I will have more to say about the weaknesses of elections in curbing ethical abuse in chapter 6.

Political scientists have been more eager than economists in embracing the virtues of regulation as a means of thwarting opportunism. The reluctance of many economists stems in part from the effects that government intervention can have on the rational behavior and expectations of consumers and producers, but George Akerlof (1970) sees government regulation (for instance, in the form of licenses) as a viable mechanism for reducing opportunism resulting from consumer ignorance. In politics, the parallel to regulation and licensing as mechanisms for controlling opportunism would probably be ethics codes.

In many cases, ethics codes provide monitoring features (e.g., financial disclosure), penalties, mechanisms for charging individuals with transgressions, descriptions of offenses, and the like. Obviously, such codes cannot possibly cover all aspects of the dealings of legislators that invite opportunistic conduct. For example, there were no specific ethical codes covering legislator transactions at the House bank prior to its dissolution. Moreover, ethics codes may give voters a false sense of security about the propriety of their legislators. "The more the law protects against fraud, the more people think the law protects against fraud," one noted economist has observed (Nelson 1974, 750). Indeed, the value of ethics codes in constraining opportunism is debatable: there seems little drop-off in the number of House incumbents found guilty of ethics violations after major ethics reforms were enacted (table 1.5). And, as the time line displayed in figure 1.1 reveals, most congressional reforms occur *after* some major scandal has transpired. Ethics reforms seem to be at best ex post responses to opportunism, rather than ex ante guards against it. One reason why ethics codes seem to have such a modest effect is because punishing unethical behavior is not a high priority for most legislators, and the infrequency and leniency of the punishments are unlikely to scare off many opportunistic legislators.

Congress has two major sanctions available: expulsion and censure. Expulsion is by far the more severe form of punishment and is normally reserved for truly dastardly behavior (e.g., acceptance of bribes as in the Abscam investigation in 1980). For offenses where expulsion is viewed as too severe, Congress punishes its members by reprimanding them in

TABLE 1.5
Ethics Violations by House Incumbents after Enactment of Stronger Ethics
Codes: 1958–1990

1958 Code of Ethics Violations: 1958–1977	1978 Ethics in Government Act Violations: 1978–1988	1989 Ethics Reform Act Violations: 1989–1990
D. Brewster (D-Md.)	D. Flood (D-Pa.)	H. Ford (D-Tenn.)
E. Garmatz (D-Md.)	J. Jenrette (D-S.C.)	N. Gingrich (R-Ga.)
A. C. Powell (D-N.Y.)	R. Lederer (D-Pa.)	
T. Johnson (D-Md.)	J. Murphy (D-N.Y.)	
F. Boykin (D-Ala.)	M. "Ozzie" Myers (D-Pa.)	
H. Addonizio (D-N.J.)	F. Thompson (D-N.J.)	
J. Dowdy (D-Tex.)	R. Kelly (R-Fla.)	
M. McKneally (R-N.Y.)	M. Biaggi (D-N.Y.)	
C. Gallagher (D-N.J.)	R. Garcia (D-N.Y.)	
J. Whalley (R-Pa.)	F. Clark (D-Pa.)	
B. Podell (D-N.Y.)	J. Eilberg (D-Pa.)	
F. Brasco (D-N.Y.)	F. Richmond (D-N.Y.)	
A. Roncallo (R-N.Y.)	J. Weaver (D-Ore.)	
A. Hinshaw (R-Calif.)	G. Ferraro (D-N.Y.)	
W. Wyatt (R-Ore.)	M. Oakar (D-Ohio)	
H. Helstroski (D-N.J.)	R. Stallings (D-Idaho)	
J. Hastings (R-N.Y.)	A. Murphy (D-Pa.)	
	J. Wright (D-Tex.)	
	T. Coelho (D-Ca.)	
	P. Swindall (R-Ga.)	
	C. Rose (D-N.C.)	

Source: Compiled by author from *Congressional Ethics* (Congressional Quarterly, 1992).

a legislative resolution of censure; expulsion forces a member to vacate his or her seat in Congress. In the Senate, censure proceedings are carried out more moderately than they are in the House of Representatives. The senator accused of wrongdoing, for example, is allowed to speak in his or her own defense. The House treats the accused with far less dignity and civility. Not only are alleged offenders often denied the privilege of addressing the chamber, but censured members are treated like felons appearing before a judge: the Speaker of the House calls the person to the front of the House chamber and issues a solemn pronouncement of censure.

Recently, a third form of punishment has materialized: the reprimand. Although there may not be much of a difference between censure and reprimand in terms of substance, there are some features of a congressional reprimand that make the punishment less annoying. For example, the member targeted for reprimand need not be present to hear the

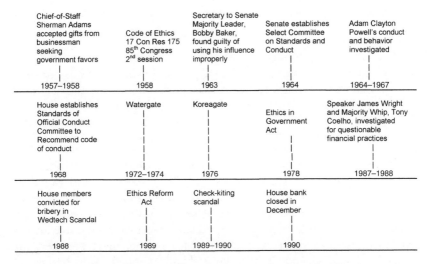

Figure 1.1 Chronology of Scandals Surrounding Ethics Reforms in the U.S. Congress: 1958–1990. *Source*: Compiled by author from *Congressional Quarterly* (Congressional Quarterly, 1992).

reprimand, unlike with censure where the censured party is publicly admonished. The absence of public humiliation makes reprimand a weaker form of punishment. In fact, former Senate Ethics Committee Chairman, John Stennis (D-Miss.), referred to reprimand as meaning little: "It just does not mean anything. It means what you might call a slap on the wrists. It does not carry any weight" (*Congressional Ethics* 1992, 45). The inclusion of reprimand in the arsenal of congressional punishments seems to accomplish little except to weaken further the punishments already available by adding another modest form of denouncement.

Irrespective of the severity of these punishments, opportunistic legislators need not be overly concerned since there is a reasonable likelihood of escaping congressional sanctions altogether. Over the years, legislators have faced a greater likelihood of being excluded from the House (31.3%) than of being expelled (14.3%), and nearly 40 percent of those subjected to a censure vote escaped punishment (Parker 1996, 148, figure 17). Although legislators found guilty of violating congressional rules always face the possibility of punishment, the risk is not too imposing.

Another reason why ethical codes seem so ineffective is because it is difficult to institute any form of informal enforcement. Many legislators see acts of questionable propriety as perfectly legitimate. For example, despite federal law prohibiting nepotism, members of Congress do not see the hiring of relatives as particularly unethical:

> Many of the respondents [congressmen interviewed] reported that they saw nothing wrong with hiring a wife, husband, or brother since their relatives were apt to be knowledgeable about the districts (and the congressman's) needs as well as loyal and hardworking. They acknowledged, however, the ease with which the practice can be made to appear improper to the public eye. (Beard and Horn 1975, 11)

Moreover, even when legislators readily agree that an act is quite unethical, they perceive such actions as widely accepted and practiced (Beard and Horn 1975). The absence of potent sanctions can certainly explain why some unethical behavior seems to thrive, but equally important is the attitude of most congressional representatives: live and let live. In matters of personal and financial conduct most members are willing to tolerate, and perhaps even shield, members who happen to step out of line. Clearly, for ethics laws to be effective, they must do more than merely trap violators. They also must punish those who abrogate their responsibilities to report and discipline colleagues who violate ethics rules. Ethics laws may not be particularly successful on the first account (i.e., trapping violators), but they are even less successful on the second (i.e., punishing those who fail to report or discipline wrongdoings).

Weak formal penalties are reinforced by only weaker *informal* sanctions:

> Almost no member reported that he would reject advice on legislation from a colleague he considered to have behaved unethically. Nearly all the respondents said they would accept and indeed seek out advice from a member if he were known as an effective legislator, regardless of his ethics. A few noted that they could impose sanctions of a sort — for example, by refusing to assist a particular colleague in matters before their committee — but more said that this was often ineffective and could lead to retaliation. (Beard and Horn 1975, 67)

Obviously, the most difficult and unlikely means of disciplining congressional behavior is by having individual legislators serve as "policemen." One member can do very little on his or her own, and the effort to provide such a collective good could involve retaliation and recrimination if the accused chose to fight back legislatively and/or personally. And if we rely upon Congress, only major expressions of unethical activity will spring the institution into action. Therefore, unless public outrage or ridicule is rampant, Congress has few incentives to ferret out malfeasance and opportunism. For these reasons, the ethical behavior of legislators is difficult to police through ethics codes.

Admittedly, legislative actions (e.g., ethics codes) have effectively eliminated some quasi-ethical behaviors, like lame-duck travel and the acceptance of honoraria, but their capacity to constrain opportunism remains questionable. For one thing, enterprising legislators may find circuitous ways to avoid "ethics traps." For example, the effect of limiting lame-duck travel prompted many opportunistic legislators to indulge in foreign travel in the years immediately preceding their retirement (Parker and Powers 2002). Indeed, ethics rules may have driven opportunism to other legislative activities, or incited new subterfuges, such as "helping" people who then "help" legislators' family members. In short, ethics rules are undoubtedly overrated as mechanisms for deterring legislator opportunism. Economic solutions to opportunistic behavior may provide more viable alternatives for controlling devious conduct in politics.

SOME ECONOMIC SOLUTIONS TO OPPORTUNISM IN POLITICS

Economic remedies for opportunism seem rather easily applied to politics. For example, economists have argued that shirking can be reduced in team-production situations by employing a monitor who receives the residual rewards brought about by reducing shirking. "If owners of cooperating inputs agree with the monitor that he is to receive any residual product above prescribed amounts (hopefully, the marginal value products of the other inputs), the monitor will have an added incentive not to shirk as a monitor" (Alchian and Demsetz 1972, 782). Team-production situations create conditions conducive to shirking, since each team member is aware that his or her effort has some effect on the team's reward, but that this reward will be divided among all members; hence, the individual must bear the full cost of the effort but only receives a portion of what that effort actually produces. Shirking looks very attractive under these conditions because when the individual reduces his or her effort, thereby shirking, the savings in effort accrue only to him or her, and the resulting losses in team rewards are borne largely by other team members. Team production and rewards fall as a result, of course, and each team member may actually be worse off than if no one had engaged in shirking from the outset. But even if team members realized that their collective effort was suboptimal, this would not in itself enable them to solve this problem since any cooperative effort is plagued by a collective goods dilemma that promotes free-rider behavior among team members.

The usual market mechanism — namely, allowing non-team members to bid to replace shirking members — will not work to solve the shirking problem: bidders cannot know who the shirkers are, and perhaps worse, successful bidders would have incentives to shirk once they joined the team. The conventional way to mitigate such a shirking problem would be to monitor the productive efforts of team members. If monitoring were perfect, each team member's marginal product would be known with certainty and shirking would be completely eliminated. However, since monitoring is costly, the best that can be accomplished is to invest in monitoring up to the point where marginal costs begin to outweigh the marginal benefits gained from reduced shirking. Thus, some element of shirking is tolerated because it is too costly to do otherwise.

Alchian and Demsetz contend that the most efficient way to ensure team productivity and reduce shirking is to employ a specialist in monitoring (residual claimant) who has title to the team's residual rewards and serves as a central contracting agent with all of its members. The residual claimant would then pay members their estimated marginal product, based upon bilateral contracts with each team member, and receive the remaining amount as personal income. This gives the claimant both the incentive and the authority to adjust payments in accordance with observed productivity, and to make changes in the composition of the team in an effort to induce greater team rewards.

In politics, party leaders serve as examples of how residual claimants operate to reduce legislator shirking in the production of public policies. Party leaders can be viewed as earning "chits" (i.e., political favors) from groups and other legislators for pairing-up suppliers (e.g., committee members) with demanders (e.g., interest groups) of public policies. Like residual claimants, the more efficient and effective the legislative efforts of leaders in the production of legislation, the greater the "residual" returns they receive (Parker 1992, 55–56). That is, the fewer the chits used in passing legislation, the greater the "profits" leaders earn, thereby providing leaders with a rationale for monitoring the behavior of party members and reducing shirking in the production of legislation.

Legislative leaders operate as "monitors" in other ways to reduce opportunism on the part of their members. For instance, the nature of the legislative process provides numerous opportunities for members to renege on their promises. Such reneging can occur by legislators returning to their constituencies once their bills are passed without sticking around to carry out the quid pro quos that led to the passage of their legislation, changing votes on subsequent bills, or not working as hard as possible for the passage of others' bills. One tactic to deal with such a predicament is for party leaders to schedule final votes at the end of legislative sessions where, due to the highly publicized nature of these actions, and the short time span between vote trades, there will be few opportunities for reneging (Crain et al. 1986). As for legislators who can be counted on to keep their bargains, their bills are passed earlier in the session since the leadership knows that they can be relied upon to follow through on their bargains. "In other words, earlier and more certain passage of bills is a premium paid to those legislators who have passed through a party loyalty filter. Their differential reward is a higher expected present value for the laws they sponsor (they are more likely to be passed and to be passed sooner in final voting), with the accompanying implications of better reelection prospects and so forth" (Crain et al. 1986, 835).

It should come as no surprise that economists have advanced solutions to problems of opportunism that involve monetary incentives. One such solution envisions consumers paying producers so that the latter won't cheat them by producing low-quality rather than high-quality goods. This "extortion money" is termed the *quality-assuring price* — the price above the minimum average cost of producing a high-quality product. This "price premium" provides incentives for firms to produce high-quality goods in order to obtain a perpetual stream of quasi-rents:

> Intuitively, the quality-assuring price treats the potential value of not producing minimum quality as an explicit opportunity cost to the firm of higher quality production. Hence the quality-assuring price must not only compensate the firm for the increased average production costs incurred when quality above that detectable prior to purchase is produced, but must also yield a normal rate of return on the foregone gains from exploiting consumer ignorance. The price "premium" stream can be thought of as "protection money" paid by consumers to induce contract performance. (Klein and Leffler 1981, 624)

Klein and Leffler (1981) demonstrate that, provided there is a sufficiently high-price premium over and above the price that would obtain if quality were observable, the future stream of profits from producing high-quality goods is usually greater than the one-shot cost savings from producing low-quality items (i.e., cheating).

In the political sphere, Robert Barro (1973) has suggested something very similar: pay legislators salaries that are so high that the income loss that would result from electoral defeat (due to evidence of corruption in office) would be greater than the monetary value of engaging in acts of corruption; then, officeholders would substitute "public" goods for private ones. Nobel Laureates Becker and Stigler (1974, 12) agree: "Trust calls for a salary premium, not necessarily because better persons are

thereby attracted, but because higher salaries impose a cost on violations of trust." Nonetheless, even substantial increases in the salaries of
legislators have not resulted in the disappearance of opportunism or
corruption in the U.S. Congress.

A widely accepted economic solution for constraining opportunism is
some form of one-party organization or, as economists term it, vertical
integration. Opportunism is reduced by substituting administrative decisions for contractual transactions. Nobel Laureate Ronald Coase (1960,
16) characterizes the process in this way:

> Within the firm, individual bargains between the various co-operating
> factors of production are eliminated and for a market transaction is
> substituted an administrative decision. The rearrangement of produc-
> tion then takes place without the need for bargains among the owners
> of the factors of production. . . . [T]he firm would acquire the legal
> rights of all the parties, and the rearrangement of activities would not
> follow on a rearrangement of rights by contract but as a result of
> administrative decision as to how the rights should be used.

In short, vertical integration is an endogenous response to ex post contractual problems that induce opportunism. Similar conditions plague
legislative institutions: agreements are forged among autonomous agents,
but instruments to exogenously enforce such agreements are lacking;
hence, legislative agreements are subject to cheating and reneging (Shepsle
and Weingast 1987).

Indeed, Barry Weingast and William Marshall see strong parallels between the problems encountered by businesses engaged in contractual
market transactions and the problems legislators encounter in the give-
and-take of legislative bargaining:

> A variety of exchange problems arise because the value of today's
> legislation significantly depends on next year's legislative events.
> Members of future sessions face incentives different from those faced
> when the trade occurred and may seek, for example, to amend, abol-
> ish, or simply ignore previous agreements. . . . In the face of uncer-
> tainty over the future status of today's bargain, therefore, legislators
> will devise institutions for long-term durability of agreements that
> ensure the flow of benefits beyond this session of the legislature. (Wein-
> gast and Marshall 1988, 138–139)

Weingast and Marshall argue that legislatures devise a form of vertical
integration for preventing ex post reneging on legislator IOUs, enforcing legislative bargains, and ensuring the durability of the latter. The
committee system accomplishes these objectives by allocating agenda

control to each committee, thereby enabling them to exercise a virtual veto over the policy proposals of noncommittee members. Restricted access to the legislative agenda discourages ex post reneging. Each committee, therefore, controls the fate of its own proposals, and no committee has an incentive to upset this arrangement. In essence, legislators give up their own influence over the fate of proposals in other committees (jurisdictions), in exchange for exclusive control over policies in the jurisdiction of their committees.[3] Committees, from this perspective, control all aspects of policymaking in a particular area (e.g., proposal, amendment) which gives them the same type of centralized authority that firms obtain through vertical integration (for example, control over inputs).

In economics, one major alternative to vertical integration as a solution to opportunistic behavior is some form of enforceable long-term contract. Such long-term contracts are either explicitly stated contractual guarantees legally enforced by government, or implicitly enforced by market mechanisms that entail the withdrawal of future business if opportunistic behavior occurs. While explicit long-term contracts can solve opportunistic problems, they are frequently very expensive solutions since they involve costs such as specifying possible contingencies, detecting violations, and enforcing contractual provisions. Because every contingency cannot be cheaply specified in a contract, or perhaps even known, and because legal redress is normally expensive, firms find it rational to also establish an implicit type of long-term contract that employs a market rather than a legal enforcement mechanism — that is, the imposition of a capital loss by the withdrawal of future business. Indeed, most firms rely upon the loss of future business as a means of preventing post-contractual opportunism (Klein et al. 1978).

This extralegal market sanction provides incentives for individuals to adhere to agreements in order to maintain a flow of benefits over time. Adam Smith was one of the earliest economists to recognize "the discipline of continuous dealings":

A dealer is afraid of losing his character, and is scrupulous in observing every engagement. When a person makes perhaps 20 contracts in a day, he cannot gain so much by endeavoring to impose on his neighbors, as the very appearance of a cheat would make him lose. Where people seldom deal with one another, we find that they are somewhat disposed to cheat, because they can gain more by a smart trick than they can lose by the injury which it does their character. . . . [W]herever dealings are frequent, a man does not expect to gain so much by any one contract as by probity and punctuality in the whole, and a prudent dealer, who is sensible of his real interests, would rather choose to lose what he has a right to than give any ground for suspicion. (Smith 1997, 17–18)

In legislatures, this is a useful way to encourage contractual compliance, but it is probably insufficient in deterring opportunism. "It is well known, however," Weingast and Marshall (1988, 142) caution, "that 'the long arm of the future' is inadequate in settings in which agents have private information and in which it is impossible or too costly to specify all contingencies in advance." Unfortunately, such conditions— private information and numerous contingencies—mark most legislator transactions.

For some consumers, anxieties are eased, and misgiving about a product allayed, by "warranties." Warranties are often heralded as means for assuring the quality of goods by reducing the incentives for providing "defective" products. Theoretically, if a warranty exists, whenever a product fails the firm has to make a payment that is greater than the cost savings of producing the low-quality good. Still, many products break not only due to poor quality, but also because consumers do not look after them properly—a level of care that is unobservable to the business producing the good. In short, in many cases it cannot be established convincingly whether a product failed because it was of poor quality, or because it was poorly maintained (for a good discussion of warranties, see Allen 1984, 323–327). Thus, ironically, the payment necessary to entice businesses to produce quality goods (i.e., warranties) may destroy the incentives for consumers to look after the product! As a result, firms will eschew full warranties in favor of partial ones.

If warranties constitute only partial solutions to cheating, what then ensures businesses will continue to produce high-quality goods? In such cases, threats to reputational capital are necessary to ensure the production of high-quality goods. For instance, a television may have a one-year guarantee, but the consumer is expecting a lifetime of ten years from it. Reputation rather than warranty provides the seller with an incentive to produce a television that lasts ten years. Perfect guarantees may be impossible, but reputability supplies an implicit assurance of performance: cheating on product quality can result in declines in consumer goodwill which translate into losses in wealth. This occurs, in part, because reputations are bonded so that misfeasance is punished by losses, for example, in future business and existing capital.

Thus, one important feature of reputations that makes them capable of constraining opportunism is their capacity to function as performance bonds. Klein and Leffler (1981) incorporate this notion of performance bonds into a competitive market model where businesses that produce low-quality goods, but nonetheless sell them at prices reserved for high-quality items, acquire bad reputations; they are then boycotted by discerning consumers, thereby ruining the earning power of the business's brand name. Firms that cheat their customers don't merely lose sales in the future; they also risk more immediate losses in the value of the firm's sunk investments, losses that may be substantial. For example, "initial press reports of allegations or investigations of corporate fraud against private parties correspond to an average decrease of 1.34 percent, or $60.8 million, in the values of the common stock of affected companies. For frauds against government agencies, the loss in value is 5.05 percent, or $40.0 million. These losses are too large to attribute to expectations of impending legal sanctions" (Karpoff and Lott 1993, 759).

Thus, brand-name capital serves as an explicit hostage to prevent cheating from occurring. In this way, a business's reputation is an investment, and a soiled brand name represents a real economic loss. So, too, in politics. How exactly reputations encourage honesty in politics and deter unethical conduct is discussed in the next chapter.

CONCLUSION

The role of reputations in this inquiry conforms to what might be termed "business mythology." This mythology argues that danger to quality is a consequence of the intrusion of "upstarts" and "fly-by-nights" who are only in the market for a quick gain. Established businesses, in contrast, with reputations to protect, and therefore a long-term horizon over which to discount their returns, realize the necessity of maintaining quality standards. "In a market with many sellers with varying discount rates, and thus varying propensities to sell reliable products, the consumer has an incentive to classify traders by discount rate, and traders with low discount rates have an incentive to reveal themselves as such, for example, by emphasizing the established nature of their business" (Heal 1976, 502). Likewise, politicians with sterling reputations have incentives to trumpet that fact.

CHAPTER 2

How Reputations Control Cheating in Economics and Politics

DECEPTION IS HARDLY UNIQUE to politics. Children and teenagers lie to their parents; students fabricate excuses; and advertisers mislead consumers. In each of these relationships effective means exist to moderate untruths: parents can "ground" their children, teachers can assign failing grades, and deceived consumers can sue. These explicit sanctions make up an important part of the costs of deception and dishonesty, but equally important is the loss of reputational capital. The need to appear reputable is essential in those instances where direct penalties for dishonesty (e.g., lawsuits or bond forfeitures) are costly to enforce or otherwise unavailable. Reputability pays off in a number of other ways. In the market, favorable reputations enable firms to charge premium prices (Klein and Leffler 1981), attract better job applicants (Stigler 1962), enhance their access to capital markets (Beatty and Ritter 1986), and attract investors (Milgrom and Roberts 1986). Reputations in politics can have similar positive effects, especially in constraining unethical behavior.

The purpose of this chapter is not merely to summarize current economic thinking about reputations; far more than a meager chapter would be necessary for that endeavor. Rather, the focus is on the properties of reputations that appear to account for the reluctance of businesses to cheat unknowing consumers. Once I have identified these features, and given them political relevance, I then explore the extent to which these reputational controls face obstacles in Congress (chapter 3). Here I am concerned with describing three conditions or incentives that make reputations, directly or indirectly, important in controlling opportunism on the part of politicians and businesses: discerning consumers (or voters) who share their experiences with others; the potential loss of reputational capital if unethical behavior is uncovered (i.e., nonsalvageable capital); and quasi-rents (i.e., premiums) to assure honesty.[1] There are undoubtedly other properties of reputations that deter cheating, but the above three features appear to be prominent in the economics literature, and are relevant to politics, as I hope to demonstrate. In any event, the study of these reputational incentives provides a good beginning for assessing the capacity of reputational controls to constrain unethical behavior in legislatures.

In addition to these three incentives, there are two other properties of reputations that aid in understanding why reputability constrains cheating: rationality on the part of consumers (voters) and producers (politicians), and the capacity of reputations to serve as information shortcuts. I discuss these latter two properties first. For analytic reasons, I will refer to these five conditions or properties of reputations as assumptions. These properties create a structure of incentives that discourage cheating in politics and markets.

RATIONALITY

A fundamental assumption in economic theory and rational-choice models of political behavior is that rational individuals seek to obtain objectives with the least expenditure of personal resources. Admittedly, criticisms of the rationality assumption are becoming more frequent, but not to the point of threatening its prevalence in economic theory and derivative paradigms. Furthermore, considerable empirical evidence could be mustered in support of this assumption. Regardless of its virtues, the value of any assumption should not be considered in the abstract, but rather in terms of its relevance for understanding a specific problem. And, indeed, this assumption helps to explain why opportunism occurs. For example, rational legislators will not make large investments in a reputation as a trustworthy and dedicated public servant if such investments do not yield sizeable returns to compensate them for the sacrifices and costs incurred. Consequently, with less invested, the costs to unethical conduct look less daunting.

The rationality assumption implies that voters and politicians seek to accomplish their highest-ranked objectives at the least possible cost, and when choosing among alternatives that yield equal benefits, they select the cheapest option.

> A rational man is one who behaves as follows: (1) he can always make a decision when confronted with a range of alternatives; (2) he ranks all the alternatives facing him in order of his preference in such a way that each is either preferred to, indifferent to, or inferior to each other; (3) his preference ranking is transitive; (4) he always chooses from among the possible alternatives that which ranks highest in his preference ordering; and (5) he always makes the same decision each time he is confronted with the same alternatives. (Downs 1957, 6)

In short, rational politicians and voters want to accomplish their goals in the cheapest manner possible. Reputations serve this purpose by conveying information in a very succinct fashion. Politicians gain because they can engender support by simply repeating the reputational associations in communications and interactions with voters. Voters benefit by obtaining information about their politicians in a concise, and easy to digest, manner.

INFORMATION SHORTCUTS

The second assumption is based on the observation that consumers seek to economize on the acquisition of information (see, for instance, Stigler 1961, and Nelson 1970). If so, we can then expect rational voters to seek informational shortcuts about politics, policies, and the behavior of politicians. Such shortcuts may be the only way for voters to make any sense of politics:

> Voters do not know in great detail what the decisions of the government are, and they cannot find out except at a significant cost. Even if they did know, they could not always predict where a given decision would lead. Therefore, they would be unable to trace the consequences of each decision accurately. . . . Nor do they know in advance what problems the government is likely to face in the coming election period. (Downs 1957, 98)

Here, again, voters seem to confront the same dilemmas as consumers. "Consumers are continually making choices among products, the consequences of which they are but dimly aware. Not only do consumers lack full information about the prices of goods, but their information is probably even poorer about the quality variation of products simply because the latter information is more difficult to obtain" (Nelson 1970, 311). Voters also lack full information about how their politicians actually stand on various policy issues, aside from what politicians say, and they are unable to predict with any degree of confidence how the latter will vote or behave in the future.

Such uncertainty drives voters, like consumers, to seek cost-saving devices to understand and predict political behavior. Voters find politics enormously complex anyway, and the existence of uncertainty just renders politics even more difficult to fathom. Voters want to know what their representatives and senators are doing in Washington, but the high costs of monitoring the actions of legislators, and the difficulty in obtaining reliable information about them, encourage voters to seek shortcuts. The absence of such shortcuts makes it virtually impossible for

voters to predict the actions of political elites and adds further slack to
the principal–agent relationship that epitomizes representation in the
United States (Kalt and Zupan 1990). In sum, the complexity of politics,
and the uncertainty surrounding political decisionmaking, force voters to
rely upon shortcuts in interpreting politics and predicting behavior.

As in economics, reputations help voters, like consumers, to economize
on the acquisition of information, especially the search for information:

> [R]eputation commands a price (or exacts a penalty) because it econ-
> omizes on search. When economists deplore the reliance of the con-
> sumer on reputation — although they choose the articles they read
> (and their colleagues) in good part on this basis — they implicitly as-
> sume that the consumer has a large laboratory, ready to deliver cur-
> rent information quickly and gratuitously. (Stigler 1961, 224)

Such shortcuts are rational information-gathering devices only if they
are correlated with the behavior of politicians; then they serve as reliable predictors of legislator behavior. If, on the other hand, these shortcuts bear little or no relationship to behavior, then voters gain little
from their use — they are simply words. In short, informational shortcuts reduce the costs of acquiring information about politics and politicians, and bear a strong correlation with the behavior of politicians.
Only cost-saving devices that meet these criteria are considered rational,
information-gathering shortcuts for voters. Reputations meet these standards quite well.

The assumption about shortcuts to acquiring information is derivative of another assumption that has played a central position in rational-choice models: rational ignorance. Most citizens realize that their
vote is unlikely to be decisive in the outcomes of the election; hence,
voters face weak incentives to acquire costly information. Downs
(1957, 245) refers to the voter's estimate of his or her *vote value* as
creating a "diminished incentive for voters to acquire political information before voting. No matter how significant a difference between parties is revealed to the rational citizen by his free information, or how
uncertain he is about which party to support, he realizes that his vote
has almost no chance of influencing the outcome." Most voters address
this dilemma by relying upon information supplied to them through the
mass media, conversations with friends and associates, newspapers, and
political advertising. "Every society provides its members with a con-
stant flow of free information about a variety of subjects. This practice
results from the face-to-face contacts in all cultures and the need for
close personal cooperation in production, leisure activities, the rearing
of children, and political action. It may also have psychological roots in
the inquisitiveness of man and his need for personal relationships with

others" (Downs 1957, 221). Obviously, no information acquisition is completely costless, since viewing the television, talking to friends, and assimilating information entail opportunity costs that must be borne by the individual consuming the information. Nonetheless, there are other costs associated with the acquisition of information that can be shifted to others, thereby making information obtained through these means as close to "free" as is conceivable.

The premise behind the assumption of rational ignorance is consistent with the assumption guiding my analysis (i.e., voters seek shortcuts that enable them to minimize the costs of acquiring and evaluating political information). As Downs (1957, 228) acknowledges, there are numerous ways to minimize the costs of acquiring information (reduce the quantity of information received, reduce procurement costs by utilizing free information, accept information produced or subsidized by commercial advertisers or the government, delegate the making of the political decision to others), although he does not specifically mention the development of reputations per se as informational shortcuts. The differences between the two assumptions are indeed modest. My rationale for assuming that voters seek informational shortcuts rather than merely minimize the acquisition of information is to draw attention to the significance of the information contained in reputations. In any event, if voters want to minimize their investments in information due to rational ignorance, or to obtain shortcuts to evaluating politicians, reliance upon reputations adequately serves both purposes.

The Extended Dealings of Businesses and Politicians

Most voters obtain information about businesses and politicians by gathering information themselves, drawing informally on the knowledge of others, or acquiring information from the politicians or businesses themselves. Information of this nature is often transmitted through "gossip" or "chatting." "Gossip is informal, private communication between an individual and a small selected audience concerning the conduct of absent persons or events. Gossip thrives when the facts are uncertain, neither publicly known nor easily discovered" (Merry 1997, 51). Gossip is simply a vehicle for storing and retrieving information about businesses, leaders, and politicians in one's community that circulates among family, friends, acquaintances, neighbors, and co-workers, and takes the form of chatting, small group meetings, correspondence, bulletin boards, leaflets, e-mail, and the like. Viewed in this vein, gossip serves to classify businesses and individuals into categories, such as trustworthy or dishonest, with new pieces of information added to the existing body of knowledge about them. In this way, gossip creates dossiers.

With respect to politics, some gossip emerges as a result of the personal experiences of voters with politicians. As a consequence of the standard free-rider phenomenon, the returns to constituents from the acquisition of information about their politicians will normally be quite small; hence, few voters will go out of their way to obtain such information. Thus, "most of their political information will come as a by-product of other activities: reading the newspaper, talking to friends, listening to sermons and television, and so forth. All of these activities are characterized by the voter's becoming informed as a member of a group" (Nelson 1976, 320). Gossip, newsletters, databanks, consumer service surveys, reporting bureaus, and referral agencies create opportunities for voters and consumers to take advantage of the information derived from personal experiences — the "extended dealings" of organizations (i.e., *dealings that are frequent with respect to a particular "promisor," and/or extended to other voters or consumers*). Stigler (1961, 219) uses a similar concept (information pooling) to describe how consumers share information on prices: "if each buyer canvasses s sellers, by combining they effectively canvass $2s$ sellers, duplications aside." Voters, like consumers, share their experiences with friends, neighbors, and co-workers. For instance, a national survey conducted in 1973 found that 91 percent of the public would "talk to friends and neighbors" about a problem, such as corruption in government, that bothered them — a percentage greater than the number who would write to their congressman or -woman (84%) or senator (81%).[2]

Table 2.1 shows how extended dealings might operate in the dissemination of information about politicians. Between 14 and 15 percent of voters report having contacted an incumbent representative or someone in the congressional office, and around 18 percent of the voters know someone who has contacted their (the respondent's) representative. Perhaps more noteworthy are the interactions between those knowing someone who has contacted their representative, and those who have contacted their own representative (see the correlation coefficients, table 2.1). Since many of those who have contacted their legislator also know of others who have done the same, it seems reasonable to conclude that a large number of these contacts are related to the intercommunication of constituents' experiences. This would not be a surprising result since the market behavior of consumers is often guided by the recommendations of friends and close associates (Nelson 1970, 361).

Clearly, information about cheating on the part of businesses must be spread to other consumers to prevent the latter from deceiving customers. "The adjustment of a seller's reputation requires both that the

TABLE 2.1
The Extended Dealings of Constituents with Their Representatives

		1978 (%)	1980 (%)	1982 (%)	1984 (%)	1986[a] (%)	1988 (%)	1990 (%)	1992 (%)	1994 (%)
Question: "Have you or anyone in your family living here ever contacted your Representative or anyone in his office?"	Yes	15.3	14.1	14.5	13.9	15.3	12.2	14.5	15.7	14.9
	No	84.7	85.9	85.5	86.1	84.7	87.8	85.5	84.3	85.1
	N =	2,255	1,377	1,211	1,757	2,132	1,654	1,970	1,343	1,484
		1978 (%)	1980 (%)	1982 (%)	1984 (%)	1986 (%)	1988 (%)	1990 (%)	1992 (%)	1994 (%)
Question: "Do you know anyone who has contacted your Representative or anyone in his office?"	Yes	19.8	12.8	19.7	17.8	20.0	17.1	18.7	19.7	18.0
	No	80.2	87.2	80.3	82.2	80.0	82.9	81.3	80.3	82.0
	N =	2,244	2,162	1,195	1,752	2,122	1,654	1,965	1,342	1,477
Pearson Correlation Coefficient between Above Questions[b]		.31	.25	.37	.49	.25	.34	.33	.35	.31

Source: National Election Studies, 1978–1994.
[a]Question asked of respondents represented by incumbents seeking reelection as well as retiring representatives in this election study.
[b]Significant at .001 level, two-tailed test of significance.

quality of his product be observable after it is purchased *and* that this information be communicated to other potential buyers" (Shapiro 1983, 664). One obvious reason why businesses are reluctant to cheat consumers is because customers who have purchased their products, only to find out that the latter fail to live up to claims, will relate their experiences to others; hence, future customers are lost along with repeat purchases. Extended dealings serve these purposes in politics as well as economics. For instance, such second-hand contact provides useful information for forming judgments about a legislator's dedication to constituency service (Cain et al. 1987, 51–57). Repeated observation that a politician's claims are true or false leads to an evolution in a politician's reputation, and if politicians believe that voters share this information, they will be reticent about engaging in opportunism, corruption, or other forms of deception (see, for example, Davis and Ferrantino 1996). Only the untrustworthy fear the spread of information among voters. "The trustworthy promisors," Klein writes (1997, 121), "welcome information sharing and, where permitted by law, will tend to organize themselves to facilitate and expand the extension of dealings."[3]

Reputational controls operate in a relatively simple way with respect to the extended dealings of businesses. Firms that cheat their customers acquire a bad reputation that is spread to other consumers who "blacklist" the firms' products. Therefore, firms have few incentives to substitue low-quality products for high-quality ones:

> When buyers have purchased a product, they discover its quality. Their evaluation eventually becomes known to other consumers through market surveys, conversations with friends, and so on. The simplest way to model this information–dissemination process, which is standard in the literature, is to assume that buyers' evaluations of the products they purchase in period t becomes known to all consumers before they purchase products in period $t + 1$. Thus, if a firm ever produces low quality, this becomes widely known, and the firm acquires a bad reputation. Once a firm has a bad reputation, consumers expect its products to be of low quality in the future and boycott the firm. (Allen 1984, 313–314)

This premise — that consumers can determine product quality after purchase and their evaluations are communicated to others — is common to economic studies of reputations (see, for example, Klein and Leffler 1981; Shapiro 1983; Fombrun and Shanley 1990).

Extended dealings on the part of voters have similar consequences in politics as in markets. First, if voters are content with their politicians, they will spread the "good word" to others, thereby increasing their politicians' support within the electorate. Second, politicians who enjoy a large extended base may attract the less informed. Voters know that a political leader with a large extended base has strong reputational incentives to behave ethically, and that evidence of propriety is a likely basis for maintaining such an extensive network of supporters. Thus, less informed voters may save themselves the costs of information by simply trusting politicians with a large clientele and an unblemished name. Bruce Cain and his colleagues (Cain et al. 1987, 150) reach a similar conclusion in their analysis of the reputations of legislators for constituency service:

> An incumbent's reputation will increase among those not helped directly, among those who do not know someone else who has been helped directly, and even among those who have not read, heard, or seen the incumbent. Perhaps some subtler reputational benefit extends beyond contacts to general hearsay.

Because politicians realize that extended dealings affect their reputations, they give considerable attention to their dealings with constituents. Not surprisingly, we find high levels of personal contact between legislators and their constituents (Parker 1986). an emphasis on constituency services (Fiorina 1977), and the maintenance of an elaborate organizational presence (e.g., district offices) within districts and states (Cain et al. 1987). It seems more than coincidence that the percentage of the personal staffs of House members located in their district offices has hovered around 40 percent, and has grown sharply. (Ornstein et al. 1996, 135). Thus, the third assumption is that reputational information is spread by consumers (or voters) who have had direct or indirect contact with politicians; hence cheating can be detected, and violations of trust spread by word-of-mouth.

Sunk Investments

Perhaps the most widely accepted conclusion about reputations is that they represent sunk costs. Individuals and firms make investments in their reputations by taking actions (e.g., entrepreneurial activity) and making decisions (e.g., advertising) that serve to foster attractive "brand names." These investments are subsequently capitalized into the reputations of economic organizations, and once capitalized, the fear of losing these sunk investments encourages firms to avoid actions or decisions that might threaten their accumulated capital. As a result, most large corporations avoid situations that cast doubt on their reputations: They remove contaminated items or products immediately from the shelves of stores; settle lawsuits out-of-court because of the damaging publicity;

and try to associate their name with worthy social causes (e.g., charities). In sum, reputations reflect investments in "capital" in the same way as corporations make investments in other more physical assets (e.g., land), with one caveat: reputations represent nonsalvageable assets.

If reputations are to serve as performance bonds, something of value must be forfeited. Reputations represent nonsalvageable assets because businesses that lose reputational capital have no way to recoup the losses. If a firm is forced to close its doors and go out of business, physical equipment, buildings, and land can be sold or salvaged, unlike the firm's reputation. Politicians, likewise, can be viewed as making investments in *human political capital* during the course of their careers in public office that they stand to lose if they engage in opportunistic or unethical behavior that results in their dismissal from office or electoral defeat. For example, they risk the loss of the entrepreneurial effort they've invested over the years in their political careers. In addition, a blemished reputation necessitates more work on an incumbent's part to stem electoral defeat, requiring larger amounts of time and effort devoted to fund-raising, campaigning, and the like, thereby detracting from more pleasurable pursuits. Thus, the fourth assumption draws attention to the sunk investments (or costs) that represent the capital invested in reputations.

Premiums for Honesty

Reputations provide a future earnings stream for both firms and politicians, the present value of which is theoretically greater than could be obtained through one-time cheating. This income stream contains a "price premium" paid to prevent cheating—a quasi-rent for honesty. As I discussed in chapter 1, one mechanism for discouraging cheating is to pay a producer a price over-and-above the competitive price—a price premium. Businesses avoid cheating under these conditions for fear of losing this quasi-rent and the enhanced income stream. The same analogy can be applied to politicians, where the premium paid to politicians consists of electoral safety and handsome post-elective employment opportunities. Politicians, like businesses, have less incentive to cheat if such cheating has detrimental consequences for their prospects for reelection and obtaining attractive post-elective employment. And this future earnings stream encompasses, of course, the valuable gains obtained as by-products of electoral safety, such as opportunities to move to committees that require greater legislator leeway, like Appropriations (Fenno 1973). Therefore, the specter of losing reelection, and perhaps any reasonable chance for prestigious post-elective employment, reduces the incentives for unethical behavior. Both legislators and businesses respond in the same way to the premiums they are paid: they avoid cheating.

Although it might be considered something of a cliché, economic actors must be motivated by personal gain. In most classical treatments of the firm or corporation, profit is the sole driving force; in politics, reelection has been viewed in a similar vein. For example, in Downs' theory of democracy (1957, 25), political parties are defined as "a team of men seeking to control the governing apparatus by gaining office in a duly constituted election." Similarly, Morris Fiorina (1977) views reelection as the primary goal of most legislators. In short, politicians have been conceptualized as largely motivated by reelection and their actions rationally driven toward that end. This is where comparisons between the economic firm and reelection-driven politicians seem problematic: while it may be profitable to maintain a brand name in the market, even if a firm plans on going out of business, politicians voluntarily exiting office have far fewer incentives to do so. Firms going out of business can redeem or salvage some of the capital invested in developing their "store of good will," but *reelection-driven* politicians are thought to have far less use for their own reputations once they have decided to leave public office. This is why last-period problems are so relevant to politics.

For politicians to behave like economic firms, they must have the same opportunity (as firms) to sell their brand names once they leave office. This can be accomplished by envisioning reputations as having relevance to post-elective employment. Simply put, reputability should help politicians acquire "good jobs" once they leave office. Serving as a legislator is a highly valued job: vast sums of wealth are spent in trying to obtain one; once obtained, members create long congressional careers; and most legislators seek reelection.[4] Upon leaving office, legislators can be expected to desire the same level of importance and prominence they received while in office, especially if their exit should be an involuntary one (i.e., lost reelection or election to a higher office). If a reputation for nonopportunistic dealings has value to potential employers, then brand names should function as they do for economic firms in restraining last-period cheating on the part of politicians.

Both reelection and attractive post-elective employment serve the same objectives for politicians—they represent job security, and a stream of future earnings. They also represent the premium paid for honesty. So, we can incorporate the more traditional view of the motivations of politicians (reelection), with the additional observation that politicians don't want to have to give up a lot in terms of prestige and importance should their political careers come to an end. I would emphasize that politicians want a "good" job, not just "work." This is, of course, their highest-ranked preference which is not always attainable; nevertheless, anything but a prestigious job is a substitute. While the assumption of job security only elaborates upon the reelection motive, it does so in an important way: *it expands the career horizons of politicians which reduces the attraction of opportunistic behavior.*

The centrality of the reelection assumption in political analyses is well-deserved, but job security entails motivations that go beyond reelection. To ignore the relevance of post-elective employment is to assure the susceptibility of legislative institutions to last-period problems. Among other things, job security means that politicians need never worry about obtaining a "good" job should they find themselves unemployed due to electoral defeat. In a sense, assurance of good employment opportunities might be viewed as akin to unemployment insurance for politicians! The effect of this proposition is to assign a longer time horizon to the motives of elected public officials by assuming that they always want to be "on top," which I interpret as remaining in office, or if they should leave office, unexpectedly or not, obtaining attractive employment. A number of considerations make employment opportunities attractive: salary, prerequisites of the job, freedom from supervision, authority, and the like. Since many politicians, especially those in Congress, possess rather unique employee benefits for which there are poor off-the-job substitutes, such as power and national or media visibility, we can expect them to value these same commodities should they ever leave or lose office.[5]

By attractive employment, I don't just mean high-paying jobs. This point is most vividly exemplified by the "downside" to high-salaried lobbying positions for former legislators. While members of Congress and senators can obtain lucrative lobbying jobs, these jobs lack the prestige and the visibility associated with legislative service. In fact, lobbying positions place former legislators in a position on the other side of the fence—they're now beholden to other legislators. They must curry the favor of others (legislators) as they were so entertained and treated when they held office. Certainly, being beholden to others for help, as lobbyists must be, is not a very attractive feature of this vocation. Although lobbyists can divert campaign monies, most incumbents are not desperate for such financial assistance since they can obtain as much campaign money as they need for their elections, and then some (Goldenberg and Traugott 1984, 59–76). Thus, only employment that rivals the prestige and visibility of political office is considered attractive. Professions held in lower repute, like lobbying, are considered less attractive no matter how financially lucrative. From the perspective of this inquiry, salary is neither a necessary nor a sufficient condition for attractive post-elective employment; prestige and visibility count for more.

There are few jobs comparable in stature to the power and authority associated with legislative service, and even prestigious post-elective employment will fall short on most accounts. There are some jobs, however, that do rival legislative service, like CEOs of major business enterprises; in the political sphere, appointment as an ambassador comes to mind. In short, the question of post-elective employment is not merely a matter of dollars. I have no doubt that legislators can earn high incomes once they leave congressional service by serving in some capacity as lobbyists, and there is an undeniable demand for these skills in today's rent-seeking society. Trustworthy or not, legislators can probably always find someone to employ them as lobbyists. For reputational controls to be effective, legislators must want much more.

One conceptual benefit derived from the assumption that premiums are paid honest politicians in terms of job security is that it incorporates *both* the reelection motive and the notion that politicians seek guarantees that they will always have attractive post-career employment opportunities. The only modification that the latter makes to the former (reelection) is to extend the politicians' motives from the immediate to the distant future. That is, politicians not only consider reelection but also what they might be doing if they should perchance lose reelection, or retire from public service; the latter two issues raise questions of post-elective employment opportunities.

IMPLICATIONS FOR LEGISLATORS' REPUTATIONS

Since the empirical focus of this inquiry is on members of Congress and senators, the question naturally arises as to how these assumptions specifically apply to legislators' reputations and their ability to constrain unethical behavior. The idea of reputations operating in the market (or even politics) makes sense only in a world of imperfect information. If the attributes of products were perfectly observable prior to purchase, then previous production of high-quality items ("brand name") would never enter the consumer's evaluations of a firm's product. Instead, consumers could derive their estimates of quality solely on the basis of personal inspection. When product attributes are difficult to observe before purchase, consumers are forced to rely upon a firm's reputation which incorporates the goodwill derived from the previous production of quality goods as an indicator of present or future quality. The uncertainty facing voters also necessitates the use of reputations, since voters lack information about the future ethical performance of their legislators, or even a remote idea about the private gain that could be expropriated through public office and lawmaking (e.g., rents).

The five assumptions, taken collectively, imply that legislators who both cultivate and sustain reputations for honesty and conscientiousness are self-policed, and are therefore unlikely to engage in unethical or quasi-ethical activities. Such "faithful agents" (i.e., trustworthy and dutiful legislators) behave ethically in part because they are rewarded with electoral safety and prestigious job opportunities once they leave Congress. This is the "premium" paid faithful agents. Faithful agents fare so well because trustworthiness is a highly regarded commodity. Table 2.2 presents data from opinion surveys of Floridians who were asked what they felt was the most important characteristic for a Representative to possess; the substantive nature of the responses for the individual categories is described in appendix 1. Floridians overwhelmingly believe that their legislators should be trustworthy. I suspect that the preferences of Floridians for faithful legislative agents would be repeated in most state and national surveys.

Validating one's trustworthiness to the satisfaction of voters requires legislators to continuously forego opportunities for personal gain. Each foregone opportunity represents a sunk cost, which is observable (in theory), and specific to the "production" of legislator trustworthiness and honesty; these costs serve as signals of "quality" (Shapiro 1983, 662). Faithful agents eschew opportunistic and corrupt behavior because, if uncovered, such actions could destroy the capital invested (sunk costs) in their reputations as well as the premiums they hope to obtain. Rational legislators can be expected to forego immediate gain if they anticipate that a profitable stream of future returns can be obtained by abstaining from unethical or quasi-legal activities.

The premiums paid trustworthy legislators include an impressive array of returns, like electoral safety and attractive post-elective employment upon leaving Congress. Voters value faithful agents and can be expected to reward them with reelection time and time again. As more and more voters learn about their legislators' trustworthiness, through personal or secondary contacts (e.g., conversations with friends), the reputations of faithful agents expand further as does their level of constituent support. In addition, faithful legislators can look forward to prestigious jobs upon their departures from Congress since employers also value the attributes associated with such agents. It would appear that there are ample incentives for legislators, like firms, to behave honestly. Thus, legislators make investments in their reputations in anticipation of obtaining these future returns. Over the long haul, these investments are capitalized into a legislator's reputation or brand name.

Table 2.2
Most Important Characteristic for Legislators to Possess

Attribute[a]	1997 Survey[b] (%)	1999 Survey[c] (%)
Trust	68.1	67.0
Service	18.3	13.0
Performance	5.5	5.0
Personal Characteristics	6.7	11.4
Issues	1.0	2.3
Religion	0.3	1.3
Number of Cases	596	616

Source: Survey Research Laboratory, Florida State University, 1997 and 1999. See appendix 1 for a description of the survey responses for each category.

[a]Question: "In your opinion, what is the most important characteristic an elected official should have to be a good representative?"

[b]Asked only of respondents who gave an evaluation of their representative; excludes respondents who didn't know who the representative was or could not evaluate him or her.

[c]Asked of all survey respondents.

The gains from reputational goodwill may extend so far into the future that they serve to further increase the incentives for ethical conduct. For example, children who follow in their politician-parent's footsteps inherit, at least initially, their father's or mother's public reputation. In a private marketplace, brand-name loyalty occurs because consumers use brand names as screening devices for product quality. Similarly, since the politician-parent is a supplier of legislative and bureaucratic unsticking services (Fiorina 1977), his or her effectiveness in that capacity, loyalty to voters, and public and private images, affect voters' perceptions. The child who follows in his or her politician-parent's footsteps inherits that reputation. In both economics and politics, "rents associated with the family name because of consumer loyalty may accrue to progeny who locate in occupations which permit full or partial capture of those rents" (Laband and Lentz 1985, 398). With respect to politics, name-brand legacies place followers at a decided comparative electoral (campaign) advantage relative to nonfollowers, who must purchase that name recognition and voter loyalty. As a result, sons of former politicians generally, and sons of congressmen in particular, exhibit greater electoral success than do first-generation politicians (Laband and Lentz 1985, 402–410). This extends the career horizons of politicians, and reduces the attraction of short-term gain and unethical or opportunistic behavior:

[T]he value of the name brand legacy which they hope to leave is substantial enough to discipline the behavior of fathers in such a fashion as to constrain them from exploiting their agency position vis-a-vis their constituents. . . . politician/father's *invest* in creation of the political legacy to be passed onto their children. This investment, in politics, takes the form of longer and more attentive service to the public than they would provide in the absence of a legacy motive. (Laband and Lentz 1985, 411)

Conclusion

Taken separately, or in conjunction with one another, the five assumptions described in this chapter suggest the following. Politicians will make investments in their reputations for trustworthiness as long as the costs of doing so do not outweigh the returns. They are motivated to make such investments because it enhances their opportunities for electoral safety and post-elective employment. Cheating customers rarely makes sense since it could result in the loss of reputational capital — sunk investments — and although monitoring is costly, the extended dealings of politicians reduce the likelihood that cheating and shirking will go undetected, or unpunished! Voters are not at all reticent about sharing their experiences (with politicians) with friends, relatives, co-workers, and other interested individuals. Constituents pay attention to the reputations associated with politicians because they convey information pertinent to evaluating their elected officials in a relatively succinct and costless way. Thus, reputations possess properties that reduce the incentives for cheating in politics and the market. This conclusion must be tempered somewhat when discussing legislators' reputations because conditions exist that mitigate these incentives for ethical conduct in Congress. In the next chapter I discuss some of these disincentives.

Lott and Davis (1992) have chided economists for being too quick to apply their models of the firm to explain the behavior of politicians. They view brand names in politics as a perfect example of how hazardous it is to compare the characteristics of the firm to the behavior of politicians:

One important difference between firms and politicians is the ability to resell this sunk investment which guarantees performance [i.e., reputations]. While a retiring owner of a firm will not cheat in his last period, since it will reduce how much he can sell his firm's brand name for, evidence indicates that politicians are much more limited in their ability to resell their political reputation. . . . The vast majority of politicians do not pass on their brand name to their offspring . . .

and endorsements provide only a partial method of transferring reputation — there is a huge difference between being endorsed by Ronald Reagan for the Presidency and running *as* Ronald Reagan. (475)

Lott and Davis are no doubt correct in urging caution in the application of principles drawn from the study of the firm to the explanation of political behavior. However, we should also be aware that *differences* between the behavior of politicians and firms may be exaggerated. For instance, as will be clear from the analysis in chapter 6, politicians can use their reputations for nonopportunistic dealings to obtain post-elective employment. In this case, politicians, like firms, behave similarly — neither has an incentive to cheat in the last period since it only reduces future earnings. It seems reasonable to expect that the honesty of both politicians and businesses earns quasi-rents.

This is not to minimize the differences between firms and politicians (see, for example, Davis and Ferrantino 1996). After all, the property rights of firms are transferable but politicians cannot sell their rights to their offices; economic markets rarely entail winner-take-all decisions (Stigler 1972), unlike our electoral system; and the claims of politicians rarely can be tested, unlike the goods often available in the market (Nelson 1976). These differences make deception more attractive to politicians than firms, perhaps, and may make it more difficult to control opportunism in politics than economics. But these contrasts between political and economic markets should not lead to the simple conclusion that economic mechanisms for controlling politicians are inappropriate or ineffective. Clearly, comparisons between firms and politicians can inform us about political phenomena by drawing our attention to aspects of politics that resemble the behavior of firms; such information may be invaluable for grasping some of the nuances in political behavior and constructing testable propositions. To use the "firm" as more than an heuristic device for understanding politics is to fall victim to Lott and Davis's persuasive critique, but to ignore its value would likely truncate our understanding of how politicians behave.

CHAPTER 3

Problems in the Market for Legislators

IN THE PREVIOUS CHAPTER, I described five propositions derived from the economic study of reputations that led to the conclusion that reputability deters politicians from engaging in opportunistic behavior. Politicians might take advantage of their reputations in the final period of officeholding, but the potential for good post-elective employment reduces such last-period problems. And although the costs of monitoring and information that fall on voters might advantage politicians, these costs are diminished by voters sharing their experiences (with politicians) with other voters. In short, reputability should provide sufficient incentives to deter unethical behavior.

This chapter describes conditions that undermine or weaken the incentives associated with reputational controls. For instance, for reputational capital to constrain opportunism, legislators must fear, at the very least, the spread of adverse information, and the loss of their long-term earnings stream (i.e., reelection and attractive post-elective employment), if their transgressions become known. Unfortunately, such incentives for ethical conduct face obstacles resulting from features of the market for legislators. This market is characterized in part by: biased information, obstacles to effective monitoring, and conditions that erode the value of the premiums awarded trustworthy legislators. Such considerations alter the cost-benefit calculations that favor investment in reputational capital, thereby mitigating the effects of reputational controls in constraining unethical and quasi-ethical behavior.

INFORMATIONAL BIASES

Since they are rational, self-interested political actors (assumption 1), the information provided by legislators will be undeniably self-serving. The evidence in support of this premise is indeed impressive. For example, John Saloma (1969), analyzing printed matter sent to constituents by representatives and senators (newsletters, new releases, form letters, and policy statements), concluded that more than one-half of the representatives (55%) and senators (63%) used their written communications to enhance their own personal images and to advance their own private interests (reelection). Constituents expect to be kept informed about issues that are relevant to their concerns, and incumbents oblige them by providing such information, but they also take the opportunity to further their own interests through these communications. Diana Yiannakis's (1982) study of newsletters and press releases demonstrates exactly how adept incumbents are at fulfilling the dual objectives. Yiannakis found that 42 percent of the paragraphs in newsletters and press releases were devoted to explaining the incumbents' stands on national issues, compared with less than 10 percent to national or local information — an amount of space smaller than that allocated to claiming credit for particularized district benefits (11.6%). In short, although the messages were more than mere propaganda, the clear intent was to present the incumbent legislator in the best possible light in order to impress constituents, and they appear to do just that.

For this reason, legislators' newsletters and the like (bulk mailings) do not serve as viable instruments for assessing legislator trustworthiness. Cheating in advertising (i.e., deception) is always possible when it is difficult to validate the advertiser's claims because the characteristics of the good stressed in the advertising (e.g., honesty) may not be easily measured by the consumer (Kotowits and Mathewson 1979). Thus rational voters are unlikely to be very impressed about promises and claims made in these mailings given the self-serving nature of these communications.

Even when voters receive information about their legislator that is not ostensibly authored by the latter, most of what they hear and read has its genesis in the legislator's own congressional office. As a result, the information supplied the local press is tailored to the legislator's preferences, not the voters. Legislators want favorable press treatment at home, and the local press wants news from Washington to impress its readers. Such conditions promote a symbiotic relationship between the local press and legislators, assuring that the latter are seen in the most favorable light.

But what if voters had first-hand experiences to draw upon — are they then in any better position? Personal experience with a product provides a good basis for quality judgments in markets; is the same true of voters' experiences with their legislators? Unfortunately, there is no reason to believe that information reaching the ears of voters, resulting from personal or secondary contact with legislators, is any better suited for the purposes of constituents. *Personal contacts with legislators, like other forms of information about them, are heavily biased in favor of legislators and easily manipulated by the latter.* There is evidence of such manipulation in the personal presentations of House incumbents during their visits to their constituencies.

Voters form impressions of the character of their political leaders partially on the basis of self-disclosure on the latter's part. This is not an unusual practice in the economic sphere, since we commonly observe sellers taking every available opportunity to demonstrate the advantages of their products — conveniences, durability, special features, warranties, and the like. Politicians behave in a similar manner. With respect to members of Congress, Richard Fenno (1978, 55) writes, "So members of Congress go home to present themselves as a person and to win the accolade: 'he's a good man,' 'she's a good woman!'" These visits back home serve as opportunities for the self-disclosure of information about their activities in Washington, rationalizing such things as their policy stands and legislative voting to their constituents. Legislators are not the least bit reluctant to manipulate this information, so self-promotion often masquerades as self-disclosure.

Personal contact with constituents is a major way through which legislators cultivate perceptions of dutiful service and trustworthiness. Fenno (1978) suggests that incumbent legislators spend time in their constituencies emphasizing three personal characteristics — *qualifications*, *identification*, and *empathy* — to create impressions that they are: qualified to hold office; able to identify with the attitudes of their constituents; and can empathize with the latter's problems. These images are transmitted at each and every opportunity that a member has to communicate with potential voters and through a variety of means (newsletters, constituent mailings, organized meetings in the constituency, personal visits), but personal contact has distinct advantages. For one thing, members of Congress exercise some control over their constituency visits. This does not merely mean the timing of their visits, but also the types of people they will see, the forum in which the interactions will occur, and to a large extent the topics they will be called upon to address:

> [T]he member has some control over his explanatory agenda at home, by directing constituent attention to subjects he feels most comfortable and knowledgeable and persuasive in explaining, or by talking to each constituent group only about that which interests them in particular or by adopting a generally low-output explanatory style. (Fenno 1978, 158)

Most of the time "a member's appearances are intended to celebrate individual, group, or community achievement and thus produce only reinforcing sentiments — 'smooching,' or 'playing butter' as two members call it" (Fenno 1978, 158). Clearly, contact of this nature cannot be expected to promote conditions conducive to acquiring information relevant to assessing the trustworthiness of legislators. Voters can be too easily manipulated through their contacts with legislators.

Second, incumbents make considerable use of these personal presentations to convey the image that they care about constituents, their problems, and their frustrations. In this way, members attempt to enhance their reputations as trustworthy and dutiful agents:

> Qualification, identification, and empathy are all helpful in the building of constituent trust. To a large degree these three impressions are conveyed by the very fact of regular contact. That is, "I prove to you that I am qualified," or "I prove to you that I am one of you," or "I prove to you that I understand," by coming around frequently to let you see me, to see you and to meet with you. If, on the other hand, I failed to come home to see and be seen, to talk and be talked to, then you would have some reason to worry about trusting me. (Fenno 1978, 60)

Granted, in all sorts of personalized service, contact is essential for determining trustworthiness. For instance, personal rapport is essential in child care, counseling, schooling, and informed medical treatment. But does personal contact provide information that helps voters resolve uncertainties about the character of politicians and the latter's credibility? Is the information derived from these legislator–constituent contacts sufficient to make rational estimates of legislator trustworthiness and honesty?

Personal contact might serve as a form of self-disclosure because it is difficult for politicians to deftly deceive a large number of voters over a long period of time. "A habit of deceit is a mark of bad character, and bad character has a way of revealing itself no matter how cunning the individual" (Klein 1997, 105). In other words, you can fool some of the voters some of the time, but you can't fool all the voters all the time. Fortunately, for opportunistic legislators, the objective is somewhat more limited, and therefore easier to achieve: fool some of the voters — those they have contact with — all the time. In sum, while personal contacts may result in self-disclosure of information, it is unlikely that such contacts will illuminate any facets of character critical to legislators. It is far more reasonable to envision those contacts as enhancing reputations for trustworthiness.

Perhaps it is the highly *personal nature* of these contacts that enhances perceptions of trustworthiness. This would explain the penchant for legislators to personalize their services, such as writing unsolicited letters congratulating constituents on recent births, graduations, awards, and the like, and appearing to sign the letters in their own hand. Extended dealings lead businesses to fear the loss of reputational capital if consumers should learn of the dissatisfaction of others. Legislators have a lot less to fear from the spread of information resulting from their extended dealings since their personal contacts with constituents encourage perceptions of trustworthiness and a positive bias to the information subsequently shared among constituents. In sum, it is questionable whether the extended dealings of legislators can serve, as they do in markets, as an incentive for constraining cheating. The personal nature of legislator–voter contacts is likely to distort or bias information so that the content of the information shared among voters is rarely critical; hence, it is unlikely that constituents will acquire information that will give congressional incumbents much cause to worry. Thus, the intensely personal (and individual) contacts between voters and their legislators, as in the request and delivery of constituency services, are unlikely to create an objective audience, or even a neutral one, for judging the propriety of members of Congress. There is no such thing as immaculate perception, especially if it is based on contacts with legislators. Extended dealings are a far weaker control on the unethical behavior of legislators than they are on the opportunistic practices of businesses.

One point seems clear: constituents have very few sources of information about the faithfulness of their legislators that are not biased in a major way. In the market, competition generates information about product quality. Legislators, however, behave more like monopolists: not only do they exercise a monopoly over the delivery of constituency services, but they exercise a near-monopoly over information about their activities. And, unlike the market where businesses are chastised for selling defective products, constituents' complaints are rarely directed at their legislators' performance; rather, voters are more likely to write their legislators about their problems with the Federal bureaucracy. Anything that legislators might do in helping constituents deal with the bureaucracy gains voter approval, whether or not the matter is resolved in favor of constituents, though most are resolved to the benefit of the latter.

The key factor about constituency service that distinguishes it from the personal experiences of consumers with businesses is that legislators bear neither responsibility nor blame for what frequently irks voters—the federal bureaucracy. Businesses, on the other hand, are more likely to be held accountable and bear the blame when consumers become dissatisfied; unlike legislators they cannot effectively shift the blame to a readily available whipping boy, like the bureaucracy. Automobile companies may blame vehicle failures on car tires, but many consumers will not be persuaded, and alarm will spread and car sales will plummet.

Therefore, information resulting from personal contact, the local mass media, or incumbent mailings is biased in the same direction and provides weak incentives for ethical conduct. The information from these sources is too easily manipulated to make incumbent legislators wary that their unethical actions will be uncovered.[1] Personal contacts between legislators and their constituents may be the least easily manipulated, perhaps, but the information is still likely to be slanted to enhance perceptions of trustworthiness and faithful conduct in office.

Problems of Monitoring

The market for legislators features a principal–agent relationship between legislators and their constituents. Principal–agent relationships are indeed legion — lawyer–client, doctor–patient, broker–investor, legislator–voters, employee–employer — and reflect contractual agreements whereby the principal expects that the agent will choose actions that produce outcomes preferred by the principal. However, there is no guarantee that the agent, once hired, will in fact pursue the principal's best interests, or do so efficiently. Agents have their own interests at heart, and they are induced to pursue their principal's objectives only to the extent that the incentive structure imposed in their contracts renders such behavior advantageous. The essence of the principal's problem, therefore, is the design of just such an incentive structure. The difficulty, of course, is that information about the agent's actions and the inputs upon which they are based is not only imperfect but highly skewed in favor of the agent.

Monitoring the actions of the agent, while one plausible way of assuring that agents pursue the interests of their principals, introduces costs that make monitoring imperfect:

> If both parties to the relationship are utility maximizers there is good reason to believe that the agent will not always act in the best interests of the principal. The *principal* can limit divergences from his interest by establishing appropriate incentives for the agent and by incurring monitoring costs designed to limit the aberrant activities of the agent. In addition in some situations it will pay the *agent* to expend resources (bonding costs) to guarantee that he will not take certain actions which would harm the principal or to ensure that the principal will be compensated if he does take such actions. However, it is generally impossible for the principal or the agent at zero cost to ensure that the agent will make optimal decisions from the principal's viewpoint. In most agency relationships the principal and the agent will incur positive monitoring and bonding costs (non-pecuniary as well as pecuniary), and in addition there will be some divergence between the agent's decisions and those decisions which would maximize the welfare of the principal. (Jensen and Meckling 1976, 308)

Constituents encounter similar problems in monitoring their politician-agents:

> Public officials are in an agency relationship with their electors, and the electorate is limited, for one reason or another, in its capacity to figure out what their agent is doing and why he or she is doing it. Moreover, even if the public could observe the actions of its agents, voters do not agree on what they wish their agents to do. And, worse yet, the set of tools that voters have for rewarding and punishing the agents' behavior in office is very limited. Thus even if voters could coordinate on their best feasible strategies, their agents would nonetheless be able to secure economic rents from the relationship. (Ferejohn 1999, 133–134)

Thus, monitoring one's legislator is likely to be a costly (and imperfect) endeavor.

While monitoring costs enhance the attractiveness of faithful agents to voters and employers, such costs also reduce the incentives for politicians to emulate that behavior. The large costs associated with monitoring the behavior of politicians make criminal acts difficult to uncover and quasi-legal and unethical actions equally hidden from public view. In fact, *minor* episodes of opportunism might escape notice entirely because of the costs involved in monitoring, policing, and enforcing codes of conduct. For instance, the high costs involved in determining who is exploiting congressional prerequisites (e.g., foreign travel) may encourage legislators to exploit this prerogative.

No doubt rational politicians, when pondering whether to build up their reputations as faithful agents by ignoring opportunities for personal gain, or exploiting those same opportunities, consider the prospects of having their actions made public. Nonetheless, legislators need not worry since most of the time their actions are likely to escape effective policing:

> Political institutions, and legislatures in particular, are likely to possess many of the attributes that make the policing of policymakers by their constituents imperfect. These attributes include attenuated constituent ownership shares; the absence of easily enforceable contracts between constituent-principals and their legislator-agents; likely impediments to competition; and free-rider incentives afflicting potential monitoring by constituents. These attributes do not imply that policymakers are not monitored and policed. Rather, policing and monitoring need only be costly to lead us to expect that constituents do not select the corner solution of perfect control over their agents. (Kalt and Zupan 1990, 107–108)

In addition, there are institutional impediments to effective monitoring that shape the incentives for shirking. For example, the six-year term of senators, combined with the inevitable decay in voters' memories over time (Figlio 2000), makes shirking attractive to senators. On the other hand, if "the term of office is short, then a relatively small number of issues will be decided before the incumbent must stand for reelection, and shirking will be relatively easy to detect and punish" (Dougan and Munger 1989, 124).

ARE THE "PREMIUMS" SUFFICIENT?

Cheating is a product of weighing the costs and benefits of unethical activities. In this section I describe why the returns from reputational capital may be insufficient to ward off opportunism. Features of the market for legislators contrive to create countervailing disincentives to legislator investments in reputational capital by decreasing the attractiveness of the premiums associated with reputability. For example, the existence of less costly alternatives to a faithful-agent reputation that are electorally successful nonetheless, and the high discounting associated with the (present) value of future post-elective employment, erode the worth of the premiums paid trustworthy legislators—namely, electoral safety and good post-election employment opportunities. The value of post-elective employment may be discounted further because of the remote likelihood of electoral defeat, the possibility that retirement is preferred to post-elective employment, or the inadequate supply of good post-elective employment opportunities. Thus, even though politicians know they earn favor with voters by building a reputation as a faithful agent, and personal contact enhances perceptions of trustworthiness with relatively little effort, reputational capital may remain surprisingly low because of weak rewards.

Availability of Substitutes

From the perspective of voters inside and outside specific constituencies, employers, and even society-at-large, a faithful agent is the optimal career path for legislators to follow. But, alas, as often occurs in economics, suboptimal solutions are selected, and no single one of these "second-best solutions" is superior to any of the others (Lipsey and Lancaster 1955). The same can be said of reputations. Thus, once legislators depart from career choices supporting a faithful-agent reputation, there are a wide variety of reputations that can be selected, and still keep a legislator electorally afloat. This is one factor that accounts for the variation in reputational capital among legislators.

Reputations behave in much the same way as other scarce goods. For instance, reputations respond to the dynamics of demand: if the cost of reputability rises, the amount of reputational capital demanded declines. Moreover, the existence of "substitutes" to a faithful-agent reputation, or simply substitute reputations, assures that an increase in the cost or price of acquiring the latter reputation will enhance the attractiveness of other reputations. Normally, the demand for faithful-agent reputations would be highly inelastic due to the electoral and employment benefits they generate, but the existence of "substitutes" makes legislator demand more elastic. The more costly it is to maintain a faithful-agent reputation, the more attractive these alternatives become.

If legislators find it difficult or too costly to cultivate a reputation as a faithful agent, they may seek substitutes. For example, legislators who find it necessary to raise large sums of money because of the historically competitive nature of their congressional districts may find it difficult to persuade voters that their actions will not be influenced by interest group contributions. And, certainly, increasing media attention to the *personal* (and past) lives of politicians may make it extremely difficult to allay the fears of voters about faithful behavior in office. Under these conditions, reputational capital will be fixed at a relatively low level and legislators may develop substitute reputations that serve voters as informational shortcuts while assuring incumbents electoral support. For instance, legislators might develop reputations as ideologues which aid voters in predicting policy positions while fostering electoral support (see, for example, Dougan and Munger 1989; Lott 1987; Hinich and Munger 1996). Politicians have the skills to construct reputations that are tailored to constituent demand and serve as viable substitutes for a faithful-agent reputation. Voters in a highly Democratic stronghold, for example, may find a politician's reputation for partisanship more important than a reputation as a faithful agent. Voters may prefer "faithful agents" to represent them, but they are prepared to accept much less, and declines in the quality of candidates, and perhaps adverse selection in the candidate pool, may provide a rationale for doing so. Voters may also be willing to accept less because they are so distrusting of politicians that they expect few of them to be trustworthy.

The pervasiveness of such variation in reputations is evident in data from a 1999 survey of Floridians who were asked to select a category that best reflected the nature of their representative's reputation. The categories included partisanship, ideology, issue stands, constituency service, attachments to special interests, and trustworthiness. Table 3.1 displays the responses to this query. The only reputation that seems to

TABLE 3.1
Variation in the Reputations of Legislators: Substitutes

Basis of Reputation[a]	Percent
Partisanship and party attachments	13.5
Ideology	9.7
Issue stands	13.5
Service to the district	25.2
Trustworthiness	18.1
Service to special interests	12.9
Something else	7.1
Number of cases[b]	310

Source: Survey Research Laboratory, Florida State University, 1999.

[a]Question: "What do you think your member has a reputation for?" Asked only of respondents who expressed an awareness of their representative's reputation (as measured in question, table 3.2).

[b]54.1 percent of the cases are classified as missing (i.e., "don't know," or no response).

stand out is constituency service; shamefully, less than one in five Florida House incumbents were viewed as having a reputation for trustworthiness. Clearly, the perceived reputations of Florida's House members are wildly inconsistent with the preferences of Floridians for trustworthy or faithful agents (table 2.2). Nonetheless, Floridians do *not* seem to punish their legislators for establishing these "substitutes." In table 3.2 I report respondent *evaluations* of their representative's reputation. Those Floridians who can make an evaluation of their representative's reputation are quite accepting of it: only 10.1 percent see it in a negative light. Substitutes for trustworthiness do not appear to incite the wrath of Floridians.

The reputations of Florida legislators are quite variegated, but they seem to reflect the basic features of reputations in general, rather than peculiarities associated with Florida's legislators. Table 3.3 presents the frequencies for likes/dislikes of representatives and senators from national surveys conducted in 1988 and 1990. There is a great deal of similarity between perceptions of legislators in these national surveys, and the reputations that are perceived to characterize members of Florida's congressional delegation. It does not seem to be too great a leap to assume that these affective responses mirror the reputational messages circulated by incumbent legislators and their constituents. If so, then substitute reputations are fairly pervasive among legislators. Since voters only care about obtaining shortcuts for understanding legislator behavior (assumption 2), they are unlikely to punish legislators for developing substitute reputations, nor are they likely to discourage them from doing so.

TABLE 3.2
Respondents' Evaluations of Their Representative's Reputation

Respondent's Evaluation[a]	Percent
Positive reputation	80.7
Negative reputation	10.1
Neither positive nor negative	9.2
Number of cases[b]	347

Source: Survey Research Laboratory, Florida State University, 1999.
[a]Question: "Some politicians develop reputations as they serve in office. How about the person who represents your district in the U.S. House of Representatives in Washington, D.C. Do you think the member from you district has a positive or negative reputation, or don't you know what the member's reputation is?"
[b]48.7 percent of the cases are categorized as missing (i.e., "don't know," or no response).

This does not mean that legislators forsake the notion of trustworthiness altogether in their desire to promote a different reputation; rather, legislators advancing substitute reputations just spend more time cultivating the latter. There may be an electoral advantage to being trustworthy, rather than say ideological, but it also may be far more costly for politicians to cultivate the former rather than the latter (see, for instance, Dougan and Munger 1989, 128). Those who find it difficult or too costly to cultivate a reputation as a faithful agent, or who meet with mixed success, frequently advance substitute reputations. The logic is clear: If a faithful-agent reputation is hard to sell, try peddling a different product.

It might be persuasively argued that these substitute reputations are not really alternatives to a faithful-agent reputation but are designed to complement or supplement the latter. There are two important problems with this argument. First, the existence of complementary or even supplementary reputations (e.g., ideological, partisan identification) complicates the market signals that legislators promote through their reputations. If reputations are designed to simplify the acquisition of information for voters (assumption 2), complements and supplements — hybrid reputations — confound these market signals, thereby defeating the purpose of reputations. Moreover, the more complex the reputation, the greater the time and effort necessary to cultivate such hybrids. Second, complementary and supplementary reputations are costly in another way. Unlike a faithful-agent reputation, complements and supplements may be ultimately damaging to reputational capital. It is easy to envision complements and supplements (e.g., liberal, conservative, Democrat, Republican) that alienate large segments of a constituency, and create reputational signals that are likely to reduce trust and per-

TABLE 3.3
Images of Senators and Representatives: 1988 and 1990[a]

Content of Likes/ Dislikes[b]	1988 Election U.S. Representative		1990 Election U.S. Representative		1988 Election U.S. Senator		1990 Election U.S. Senator	
	Likes	Dislikes (%)	Likes	Dislikes (%)	Likes	Dislikes (%)	Likes	Dislikes (%)
Leadership	1	5	2	2	3	4	2	4
Experience	11	4	14	3	14	3	19	2
Constituency Service	28	11	27	11	17	9	18	12
Trust	10	12	10	19	15	12	13	14
Personal Characteristics	10	6	11	6	11	5	9	5
Party	4	15	5	14	3	16	4	15
Ideology	9	14	6	10	11	17	7	13
Domestic Issues	10	11	13	16	12	17	14	16
Foreign Policy Issues	1	3	1	3	2	4	2	4
Group Support	9	8	7	5	7	6	5	5
Miscellaneous	7	10	4	11	6	7	6	8
Cumulative Percent	100	99	100	100	101	100	99	98
N =	692	171	1,272	396	1,565	575	3,239	1,112

Source: National Election Studies, Senate Elections in Context 1988–1990 Pooled File.
[a]Includes only House incumbents running for reelection in a state with a race involving a Senate incumbent.
[b]Table entries show the percentage of all responses that fall into each category.

ceptions of faithfulness on the part of some voters. For example, conservatives are likely to be suspicious of a legislator cultivating a reputation as a die-hard, but trustworthy, liberal. Thus, hybrid reputations are unlikely to complement or supplement a faithful-agent reputation; instead, they serve more frequently as substitutes. Admittedly, legislators want voters to see their substitute reputations as complements or supplements to a faithful-agent reputation, but eventually the former become the major objects of cultivation. As if guided by Coase's theorem (1960) regarding economic behavior, the resources of legislators — their time and effort — gravitate to their most valued use in forming reputations.

If legislators develop substitutes to a faithful-agent reputation, their actions will *not* be directed toward building reputational capital in the sense described in this inquiry (i.e., sunk investments in a reputation for trustworthiness and dutiful service). The lack of reputational capital makes opportunism all the more attractive: failure to build a reputation as a faithful agent prevents legislators from capturing the returns derived from that reputation (e.g., attractive post-elective employment), thereby creating incentives for legislators to milk their reputations. Anything but a reputation for trustworthiness and service — quality — invites opportunism in political and economic markets. For example, discount clothing outlets may indeed offer name-brand items at low prices, but the goods themselves could be made with inferior materials (e.g., low-cost thread, fabric), produced with the explicit purpose of selling the name-brand goods at those outlets; higher quality materials are used in the production of the same item sold (at a higher price) at major department stores.

Discounting the Gains

Since the building of a reputation as a faithful agent requires foregoing gains in anticipation of obtaining future reelection and post-elective employment, the maintenance of that reputation requires legislators to weigh the foregone returns from quasi-ethical or unethical actions against the *expected* threat to job security. As mentioned earlier, less faithful agents will discount the returns from reputability because their poor reputations lead them to anticipate unattractive post-elective employment opportunities. Yet, even the faithful may be reluctant to make sizable investments in their reputations (for example, eschewing large campaign contributions) for several reasons: post-elective employment may not be a pressing concern due to high levels of electoral safety; post-elective employment may be irrelevant because they prefer to retire; loyal voters have a habit of screening out adverse information about their beloved politicians, so any negative publicity surrounding acts of opportunism is unlikely to have significant electoral repercussions; and there may be an insufficient supply of good jobs to provide adequate incentives to induce faithful behavior.

Politicians may minimize investments in reputational capital because they heavily discount a major benefit of a faithful-agent reputation: post-elective employment. Faithful agents are more apt to obtain attractive post-elective employment because they are good contractual risks (i.e., they keep their promises). This gives them access to high-level jobs where monitoring employee behavior is either difficult or very costly. Such jobs usually entail ample opportunities for employees to trade work for leisure in the absence of monitoring. The force of this incentive for post-elective employment depends, however, on the value attached to such employment. Politicians who are electorally safe and do not seek higher office, and those who expect to retire and therefore forgo post-elective employment, will heavily discount the returns they can obtain from future employment opportunities. Similarly, less faithful agents also have incentives for discounting their future job prospects.

The less faithful stand to lose considerably less if their opportunistic transgressions are uncovered because they have fewer sunk costs invested in their reputations. That is, the less trustworthy have taken fewer actions to validate their reputations as faithful agents, and so they have less capital invested. This lack of reputational capital makes corruption and opportunism more attractive to the less faithful, while at the same time narrowing their prospects for attractive post-elective employment. As a result, the less faithful politicians find their poor reputations sinking even lower, and as they sink lower, deterrents to further opportunistic behavior grow even weaker, along with their prospects for good jobs once they leave Congress. To rephrase Nobel Laureate Gary Becker (1968, 176), some politicians cheat "not because their basic motivation differs from that of other persons, but because their benefits and costs differ."

Unfaithful politicians therefore have additional reasons for engaging in quasi-legal and unethical actions since future returns from attractive post-elective employment must be heavily discounted. They are not stupid: the "unfaithful" do not expect to obtain attractive post-elective employment should they ever leave office. They are acutely aware that they lack the reputational capital to command attractive post-elective employment. Moreover, changes in the reputation of an unfaithful politician would require considerable avoidance of opportunities for gain, and since no *single* act of fidelity and honesty will probably be decisive in altering his or her existing reputation, the unfaithful heavily discount the returns from becoming a more faithful agent. Thus, post-elective positions do not figure highly in the calculus of unfaithful politicians. We might expect senators to invest even less than House incumbents in their reputations as faithful agents because the demand for their post-elective services is far greater; hence, they need less capital to obtain a prestigious post-elective job. Senators have obtained levels of visibility and prominence that create attractive post-elective employment opportunities, irrespective of their reputations.

As for the availability of good jobs for exiting legislators, table 3.4 sheds some light on the inadequacy of "good" post-elective employment. The data in this table classify the post-elective positions of 191 former House members. What kind of job prospects do exiting legislators face? As might be expected, post-elective employment opportunities center on lobbying — not a prestigious vocation but one that pays well. Even though I have been quite liberal in defining prestigious employment (see appendix 2), only 20 percent of these exiting House incumbents took prestigious jobs in the private sector (i.e., prestige employment in private sector or major corporate appointment). With such uninviting job prospects, the incentives to build and nurture a reputation for trustworthiness, in order to enhance the quality of post-elective

TABLE 3.4
Employment Obtained by House Members upon Their Departure from
Congress: 1984–1993[a]

Type of Post-Elective Employment	Percent
Lobbying	40
Return to prior vocation	17
Prestigious employment by federal or state government	13
Prestigious employment in the private sector	11
Major corporate appointment	9
Other	10
Number of cases	191

Source: Compiled by author from *Beyond the Hill: A Directory of Congress from 1984 to 1993* (Borders and Dockery, 1995).

employment, lose some of their appeal. As a result, many politicians make rather small investments in their reputations for propriety by only avoiding outlandish or explicitly illegal acts of self-interest. It is easy to understand why most legislators rarely go above-and-beyond minimum requirements (e.g., financial disclosures) and expectations in demonstrating their trustworthiness and conscientiousness, and why some are not adverse to occasionally milking their reputations by engaging in propitious opportunistic behavior.

Being a faithful agent is important if you ever lose office, since such legislators are probably in a better position to obtain attractive post-elective employment. Although their employment prospects are no doubt brighter, the likelihood of obtaining attractive post-elective employment remains exceedingly small. Moreover, the probability of electoral defeat (at least in the House of Representatives) is almost minuscule, and if legislators anticipate retirement, post-elective employment will be heavily discounted in comparing the benefits to building or milking reputations. There are strong reasons for legislators to discount the benefits derived from a faithful-agent reputation. In sum, the availability of substitute reputations that keep legislators electorally afloat, and the high discounting of the returns linked to a faithful-agent reputation, erode the value of the premiums awarded to trustworthy legislators, thereby making unethical conduct more attractive.

CONCLUSION

The market for legislators, then, incorporates several features that could conceivably weaken the ability of reputational capital to constrain unethical behavior. First, there is a general lack of competition in congressional elections, and, as we will see in chapter 6, many factors can influence the outcome; hence, reputational capital may not even be a necessary condition for reelection. Second, there are a large number of substitutes available to a faithful-agent reputation. Thus legislators may gain election and reelection without fulfilling the obligations associated with a faithful-agent reputation. As the costs of fulfilling such obligations rise, so does the attraction of substitute reputations. Third, the extended dealings of legislators generate positive perceptions of trustworthiness because of the intensely personalized nature of legislator–constituent contacts and the ability of legislators to control and manipulate information about themselves. Fourth, there does not appear to be a large supply of prestigious jobs for former legislators, even if we are quite liberal in what constitutes prestigious employment. This reduces the incentives to build reputational capital in order to obtain attractive post-elective employment.

Fifth, the public prefers faithful agents but seems quite accepting of substitutes. This makes substitute reputations all the more attractive to legislators. Sixth, the ability of senators to obtain attractive employment after they leave Congress, because of their prior positions of power and prominence, reduces their incentives to build large stores of reputational capital. The longer "repurchase period" for senators—that is, six-year term—probably exacerbates this problem. Finally, the high costs of monitoring and policing the activities of legislators assures them more than a modicum of invisibility; such a state of affairs can easily be exploited in unethical ways. In sum, problems in the market for legislators imply that ethical transgressions will be difficult to spot; premiums associated with trustworthiness may fail to motivate legislators to behave ethically; and biased information places legislators and their actions in the best light possible. Reputational controls face an uphill battle.

CHAPTER 4

Hypotheses, Measurement, and Data

IN THIS CHAPTER I integrate propositions about reputational incentives described in chapter 2, with observations about problems in the market for legislators, to create several hypotheses about the reputations of legislators. I then describe the sources of data used to examine these hypotheses, and the measurement of reputational capital; attention is also given to the validity of the measurement of the latter. This chapter addresses the research design issues underlying this inquiry. I begin by summarizing the assumptions or properties of reputational controls previously discussed:

1. Politicians and voters are rational, utility-maximizers.
2. Reputations shortcut the costs of acquiring information.
3. Reputational capital enhances job security, ensuring a future earnings stream that rewards honesty.
4. Reputations represent sunk costs or investments.
5. Reputational information is spread by voters who have had direct or indirect dealings with politicians.

These assumptions imply that the more politicians invest in their reputations for faithful service, the less incentive they have to engage in opportunism or unethical behavior.[1] Despite the asymmetries in information that favor incumbent politicians, their "dealings" with voters spread to other constituents. As a result, trustworthy politicians know that shirking and unethical behavior will eventually reach the ears of their constituents, thereby damaging their reputations. This limits the incentives for unethical behavior, especially since a soiled reputation severely limits job security and post-elective employment opportunities.

Nonetheless, the arguments and data presented in the previous chapter suggest that conditions for reputational control of unethical behavior confront several obstacles arising from the market for legislators. Simply put, the market for legislators reduces the incentives for ethical conduct. Sure, legislators who engage in unethical activity stand to lose reputational capital, but voter recognition of the lack of faithful performance may be more difficult to come by. For instance, first-hand experience, resulting from personal contact with legislators, will favor the latter by enhancing perceptions of trustworthiness, thereby reducing the likelihood that information adverse to legislators' reputations will spread to others. And, if electoral safety can be obtained by establishing a less costly reputation, and the supply of good jobs is almost nonexistent, why should legislators incur the costs required in building a reputation as a faithful agent? Moreover, the existence of substitute reputations—and the readiness of voters to accept them—along with the expectation of poor post-elective employment, make legislator demand for reputational capital quite elastic. These and other facets of the market for legislators discussed in the previous chapter reduce the incentives for legislators to make large investments in their reputations, thereby increasing the attraction of opportunistic endeavors.

Major Hypotheses

Four generic hypotheses are explored in this inquiry:

1. Faithful agents eschew opportunistic behavior; unethical or quasi-ethical behavior results in significant losses in reputational capital.
2. Personal and indirect contacts with constituents enhance legislator's reputations for trustworthiness.
3. Reputational capital promotes electoral safety, and improves the likelihood of obtaining attractive post-elective employment.
4. Reputational capital varies across institutions because presidents, senators, and representatives face different prospects for post-elective employment. Representatives should have the highest levels of capital, followed by senators, and then presidents.

(Specific tests of the above hypotheses are described in individual chapters.) These hypotheses are linked to the assumptions recounted above in the following ways. The assumptions that politicians are merely rational, utility-maximizers (assumption 1), and that reputations represent informational shortcuts (assumption 2), are necessary to the construction of all the hypotheses, though they are not identified with any one of them. The hypothesis that faithful agents avoid unethical behavior and risk losses in reputational capital if they engage in such behavior is related to these two assumptions but is most closely linked to assumption 4—reputations represent sunk investments. As such, legislators stand to lose these investments if they engage in unethical behavior, and their actions are uncovered. Losses of reputational capital, therefore, make faithful agents reluctant to engage in opportunistic endeavors; and if they take that risk, I expect losses in reputational capital to result. Two conditions reduce opportunism on the part of businesses: the existence of nonsalvageable capital, and prices for their products or services that are above the competitive price—a price premium. Assumptions 3 and 4 replicate these conditions: Reputations are a form of non-salvageable capital (assumption 4) that rewards trustworthy politicians with premiums for honesty — electoral safety and attractive post-elective employment opportunities (assumption 3).

I also expect personal contact between legislators and their constituents to foster perceptions of legislator trustworthiness. Such contact is easily manipulated to color perceptions of trustworthiness, which are then passed on to others. This is the "extended dealings" condition (assumption 5) at work in the market for legislators. The third hypothesis is drawn directly from the assumption that reputational capital promotes job security. This assumption leads to the hypothesis that levels of reputational capital are important to the electoral safety and attractive post-employment opportunities of senators *and* representatives. Although I do not differentiate between representatives and senators in this hypothesis, the market for legislators makes this relationship problematic for senators since the latter can obtain attractive post-elective employment no matter their levels of reputational capital; hence, they have fewer incentives than representatives to make investments in their reputations as faithful agents. Granted, investments in reputational capital may enhance the other element of job security for senators — electoral safety — but large investments in reputational capital seem unlikely to substantially alter electoral safety, and given the large sums of money spent on senate campaigns, reputational capital is likely to suffer anyway as accounts surface about campaign contributors and contributions. Thus, the null hypothesis seems quite viable, especially for senators who have a lot less need for reputational capital due to the built-in advantage of a longer "repurchase period" (i.e., a six-year term) and the prominence and power of the institution in which they serve.

The final hypothesis — that reputational capital varies across national political institutions — is primarily derivative of the third and fourth assumptions. Assumption 3 implies that electoral safety and good post-elective employment are related to one's reputation as a faithful agent; however, the sunk costs associated with such a reputation (assumption 4) force rational legislators (assumption 1) to weigh the gains from further reputational investments against their costs. Again, the market for legislators influences these calculations. One factor in these calculations is a lack of competition in the market for members of the House: Representatives enjoy more electoral safety than either presidents or senators. Since a reputation as a faithful agent comes at a price, we might anticipate that legislators have few incentives to build reputational capital, especially given the existence of barriers to the entry of competition (Parker 1992) and the viability of substitute reputations. Nonetheless, members of the House need the image of reputability to obtain attractive post-elective employment, at least more so than senators and presidents. Presidents and senators are more electorally vulnerable, but they also face far better prospects of getting a good job should they leave office voluntarily or involuntarily. Simply put, a reputation for trustworthiness means a lot less to presidents and senators because it is so difficult to sustain politically, and even if they are electorally unsuccessful, they know that a pretty good job awaits them.

Thus, I anticipate a ranking. That is, I expect representatives generally to have a greater demand for reputational capital than either presidents or senators since such goodwill is far more important to them than to either of the latter in obtaining good post-elective employment. Representatives should therefore exhibit the highest levels of reputational capital. If representatives have on average less reputational capital than senators or past presidents, the hypothesis of variation in capital across institutions will be refuted, since their relatively poor job prospects should lead House members to acquire greater reputational capital to impress private sector employers. Presidents and senators have a comparative advantage in seeking post-elective employment due to the nature of their positions, while representatives need a reputation for trustworthiness to compete in the rather limited market for good post-elective employment opportunities. And, if it isn't the outlook for attractive post-elective employment, but the electoral safety of legislators, that makes politicians less eager to invest in reputational capital, then the rankings would be just the opposite, reflecting levels of *electoral insecurity*. In the latter instance, the rankings in terms of reputational capital would be presidents, senators, and representatives. Both alternative hypotheses are examined.

MEASUREMENT OF REPUTATIONAL CAPITAL

A central point in the overall argument is that reputations for trustworthiness constrain opportunism by serving as a performance bond whereby reputational capital is sacrificed by unethical behavior. Foregone opportunities for private gain are capitalized into the brand names of politicians, creating goodwill[2] and reputational capital. But how can we measure a legislator's stock of capital? I have addressed this difficult question by measuring a legislator's level of reputational capital in terms of the (net) percentage of the congressional district (sample) that mentions an aspect of faithful representation as something liked about an incumbent legislator.

These percentages of "likes/dislikes" may underestimate the "true" proportion of constituents who see their legislators as exhibiting a faithful-agent reputation, but they have the advantage of relying upon *spontaneous recognition,* a hallmark of reputations and their transmission. Moreover, the liberal definition of "likes" and "dislikes" that qualify as attributes of faithful (or faithless) agents is likely to work in the opposite direction by broadening the percentage of voters who see their representatives in these terms. It should also be noted that the percentages are based upon the entire district sample, which includes those recognizing the legislator as well as those less informed. Clearly, reputational capital would be higher if attention were restricted to only those voters who mentioned some like or dislike about their legislators (as an expression of recognition). I have not limited the analysis in this way because I believe that such a computation would distort the impact of a reputation by exaggerating its scope and depth, and complicate comparisons across legislators.

To create these district samples, National Election Surveys between the years 1978 and 1994 were pooled together. Within each district sample, level of reputation as a faithful agent (or *net reputational capital*) was derived by subtracting the number of voters mentioning something negative about the faithfulness of their legislator's performance from those voters mentioning the faithfulness of their representative in a positive vein (see appendix 3 for a list of responses), and dividing this figure by the total number of district respondents (i.e., pooled district sample).

In the analysis of the House of Representatives, legislators from the pooled surveys were selected for analysis if their district samples were at least twenty-nine voters. At this minimum level, the sample size is, regrettably, small but still permits the calculation of reasonably unbiased statistical properties. For example, a sample size of approximately thirty cases would assure that the mean distribution of a variable would be close to normal (Korin 1975, 192).[3] (Actually, over two-thirds of the district samples have at least forty respondents.) This sample size constraint meets our purposes quite well, resulting in 211 incumbent representatives for analysis. Reducing this restriction on sample size by introducing a more lenient threshold would leave us suspicious about the reliability of our statistical estimates since questions about the normality of the distribution of cases in small samples are always present. Increasing the sample level, thereby reducing the number of legislators for analysis, would only hinder our ability to draw meaningful generalizations. This is not a problem in the analysis of the data on senators since the number of cases in a state's sample is quite large, but the latter does not permit as precise a testing of the hypotheses as can be accomplished in the analysis of the House data.[4]

We can create a panel of incumbent legislators from these data since we have repeated measurements of these legislators on a variety of behaviors relevant to this analysis, for example, reputational capital and foreign travel. These repeated measurements provide conditions for quasi-experimental analyses of the effects of reputational capital in constraining last-period problems in lame-duck travel, and assessing the impact of revelations of honoraria income on reputational capital. Quasi-experimental designs exist for situations in which complete experimental control is difficult or impossible, like situations where it is impossible to randomly assign subjects to experimental groups. The quasi-experimental approach used in the analysis conforms to a *nonequivalent control group design* (Cook and Campbell 1979, 95–147; Tuckman 1972, 117–120). This design is identical to the classic pretest-posttest control group design in all respects except for the random assignment of individuals to treatment groups. The absence of randomization means we cannot assume that all variables that might affect the dependent variable have been controlled; in experimental designs, uncontrolled variables are normally dealt with through randomization of the subjects. In this quasi-experimental design, I control or adjust for these variables statistically through an analysis of covariance. In an analysis of covariance, the effects of uncontrolled variables (covariates) are removed by a simple linear regression method, and the residual sum of squares are used to provide variance estimates.

Analysis of covariance tests the significance of the differences between the means in experimental data by taking into account, and adjusting for, initial differences in the data. The adjustments are made in this analysis, as well as most panel studies of behavioral change, by removing the effects of the initial (t_1) measurement of the dependent variable from a later measurement. The relevant question is whether the experimental group outperformed the control group on the posttest by more than would be expected on the basis of their initial (or pretest) measurement. It should be clear that by removing the effects of the initial measurement, we are controlling for all the variables that might affect the dependent variable since these variables should be related to the initial measurement of the dependent variable (t_1). By removing the initial measurement from the final measurement (t_2) of the dependent variable we are, in essence, also removing the effects of uncontrolled variables. As a result, we can isolate the impact of the "treatment effects," which are causally prior (timewise, at least) to the final measurements of the dependent variable, and determine whether the effects are significant. This research design is used in chapter 5 to assess the capacity of reputational capital to constrain quasi-ethical conduct in the U.S. House of Representatives. Such quasi-experimental designs provide demanding conditions for establishing causal effect by reducing the confounding effects of alternative explanations.

One important hypothesis tested in this inquiry is whether legislators enhance perceptions of their trustworthiness through their mere contacts with constituents (chapter 7). To research this question I construct a measure of the *perceived trustworthiness* of voters' legislators. This measure is based upon responses to four closed-ended survey questions that parallel items used in the widely recognized "Trust in Government Scale." This measure of trustworthiness is highly reliable (Parker and Parker 1993) but has not been included in national surveys to date; only two opinion surveys have included the battery of items necessary to measure perceptions of trustworthiness. Therefore, the analysis of the perceived trustworthiness of legislators as it relates to constituent contacts is confined to data gathered through opinion surveys conducted in 1988 and 1997 in Florida.[5] The following survey queries were used to form this measure:

1. Of the promises (name of leader) made when he was running for office, how many do you think he has kept — all of them, most of them, only some of them, or none of them?
2. How often do you think (name of leader) has used his position to benefit himself personally — most of the time, some of the time, rarely, or never?
3. How would you rate (name of leader) honesty — very honest, fairly honest, somewhat dishonest, or very dishonest?
4. How often do you feel you can trust (name of leader) to do what is right — almost always, most of the time, only some of the time, or never?

"Trusting" responses were considered to be: leaders kept all or most of their promises; leaders have rarely or never used their positions to benefit themselves personally; leaders are rated as very or fairly honest; and you can trust leaders almost always, or most of the time, to do what is right. The "perceived trust scale" ranges from 0 to 4, with 0 representing distrust of a leader, and 4 representing total trust in a leader.

VALIDITY OF MEASUREMENT OF REPUTATIONAL CAPITAL

While the categorization of open-ended responses is always subjective, my effort to identify trusting and distrusting comments in the measurement of reputational captial has been guided by the nature of the standard "Trust in Government" questions. The useful properties of this scale, such as its predictive validity and widespread usage, provide the rationale for using these items as a guide in classifying trusting and distrusting responses. It provides some assurance that the responses used as indicators of reputational trust reflect the same underlying concept—trust. For example, the responses categorized as reflecting untrustworthiness capture the content of the items included as measurements of distrust in the Trust in Government Scale: government officials are crooked, run by interests looking out for themselves, cannot be trusted to do what is right, and are undeniably self-interested. The following questions are normally used to create the Trust in Government Scale:

1. Do you think that people in government waste a lot of money we pay in taxes, waste some of it, or don't waste very much of it?
2. How much of the time do you think you can trust the government in Washington to do what is right—just about always, most of the time, or only some of the time?
3. Would you say the government is pretty much run by a few big interests looking out for themselves or that it is run for the benefit of all the people?
4. Do you feel that almost all of the people running the government are smart people who usually know what they are doing, or do you think that quite a few of them don't seem to know what they are doing?
5. Do you think that quite a few of the people running the government are a little crooked?

Using these questions to identify trusting and distrusting characterizations of incumbent legislators adds an element of content validity to the measurement of reputational capital: the items used to compute reputational capital reflect the content of a closely related measure of trust. The responses used in measuring reputational capital are described in appendix 3 and bear a reasonable relationship to common usage and interpretation of trustworthiness and dutiful service—additional evidence of content validity.

Aside from content validity, there is also evidence of construct, face, and predictive validity to my measurement of reputational capital (Carmines and Zeller 1979). First, I establish the construct validity of the measure—that is, the existence of significant relationships between the measurement of reputational capital and variables that should have theoretically derived positive correlations to such capital, if indeed it is measuring trustworthiness. Second, I provide evidence of face validity: the rankings of senators and representatives in terms of reputational capital, and "outside" information about their past ethical conduct; the rankings of legislators should, at the very least, distinguish between the honest and less honest and correspond to auxiliary information. Third, I demonstrate that the "likes" and "dislikes" upon which the measurement of reputational capital is based represent more than symptoms of legislator electioneering. That is, I predict that the saliency of legislator attributes and images will be unaffected by the timing of the electoral cycle because these characterizations are not merely the result of campaign messages (i.e., no correlation).

The construct validity of the measurement of net reputational capital relies upon the premise that the measure contains elements of trust. Therefore, there should be strong positive correlations between the measurement of capital, and variables conceptually and empirically related to trustworthiness. Two such variables are voters' perceptions of the helpfulness of the incumbent legislator, and the latter's performance in office. And, indeed, I found a strong correlation ($r \geq .42$) between the measurement of trustworthiness and constituent perceptions of the "helpfulness" of the incumbent legislator in separate national opinion surveys between 1978 and 1984 (Parker 1989, 184),[6] and an even stronger relationship between this measure and electoral support ($r = .60$) in a pooled analysis of these data (Parker 1989, 191). In sum, the measurement of reputational capital appears to behave as we would expect of a measure based upon perceptions of trustworthiness.

Rankings of legislators in terms of net reputational capital provide additional evidence of the validity of the measure. In this case, the face validity of the measure. These measurements of reputational capital, and the legislator rankings they produce (tables 4.1 to 4.4), are consistent with other information, such as newspaper reports and opinion surveys. For instance, Bob Graham's high level of trustworthiness is attested to by his score on the perceived trustworthiness index which is based on the opinions of his Florida constituents (see chapter 7). In addition, one of the senators who ranks highly in terms of reputational capital is Claiborne Pell (D-R.I.), and personal observation as well as considerable auxiliary information attests to Pell's high level of capital:

When asked [in 1978] to name, without any coaching, something they liked about Pell, the largest number (15%) mentioned "honest or sincere or straightforward." On a set of fourteen different traits, he scored highest on "honest" and next highest on "knowledgeable." And, on a battery of twenty-one agree/disagree statements, he received his two highest agreement scores on the statement "Pell is a thoughtful person, you can trust his judgment" (68% agreement) and on the statement "Pell is a man of character, he does the right thing" (65% agreement). . . . In his 1989 poll, on a battery of agree/disagree

TABLE 4.1
Top Twenty-Five Senators in Terms of Reputational Capital

Senate	State	Net Reputational Capital (%)
1 Bob Graham	Florida	28.7
2 Barbara Mikulski	Maryland	27.2
3 Richard Lugar	Indiana	21.2
4 Claiborne Pell	Rhode Island	19.2
5 Robert Kerrey	Nebraska	19.0
6 John Chafee	Rhode Island	18.9
7 David Boren	Oklahoma	17.9
8 Nancy Kassebaum	Kansas	17.1
9 Daniel Moynihan	New York	16.9
10 Paul Simon	Illinois	16.8
11 John Glenn	Ohio	15.9
12 Pete Domenici	New Mexico	15.5
13 William Cohen	Maine	15.5
14 John Warner	Virginia	15.1
15 John Danforth	Missouri	14.2
16 William Roth	Delaware	13.6
17 Jeff Bingaman	New Mexico	13.2
18 Slade Gorton	Washington	13.1
19 Pete Wilson	California	12.3
20 Sam Nunn	Georgia	12.1
21 George Mitchell	Maine	12.0
22 Herbert Kohl	Wisconsin	12.0
23 James Jeffords	Vermont	11.8
24 Joseph Lieberman	Connecticut	11.7
25 Dan Coats	Indiana	11.4

Source: Computed by author from National Election Studies, 1978–1994.

questions, his highest score was 70 percent constituency agreement that "Pell's integrity and honesty are above reproach." And in another battery of eight standard job performance questions, his highest ratings — 83 percent positive, 55 percent extremely positive — came on the statement that Pell is "a person of great personal character, ethics, and integrity." (Fenno 1996, 264, 272)

Some of the legislators in this analysis with the lowest levels of reputational capital appear to have well-earned reputations for opportunism, if not outright corruption. For instance, Robert Badham (R-Calif.) converted about $40,000 in leftover campaign funds for personal use, and Beryl Anthony (D-Ark.) had 109 overdrafts at the House bank.

TABLE 4.2
Lowest Twenty-Five Senators in Terms of Reputational Capital

Senate	State	Net Reputational Capital (%)
1 Joe Biden	Delaware	−5.1
2 Lowell Weicker	Connecticut	−4.7
3 Dennis DeConcini	Arizona	−3.5
4 John Melcher	Montana	−3.3
5 Steven Symms	Idaho	−2.9
6 Harris Wofford	Pennsylvania	−2.3
7 Frank Murkowski	Alaska	−2.1
8 Bob Kasten	Wisconsin	−.1
9 Spark Matsunaga	Hawaii	0.00
10 Kit Bond	Missouri	0.40
11 Paul Sarbanes	Maryland	0.90
12 Wyche Fowler	Georgia	1.3
13 Dale Bumpers	Arkansas	1.6
14 Brock Adams	Washington	2.4
15 J. Bennett Johnston	Louisiana	2.6
16 Gordon Humphrey	New Hampshire	2.7
17 Conrad Burns	Montana	2.7
18 Bob Packwood	Oregon	2.9
19 Connie Mack	Florida	3.0
20 Tom Harkin	Iowa	3.2
21 William Armstrong	Colorado	3.3
22 John Rockefeller	West Virginia	3.4
23 Alan Dixon	Illinois	3.5
24 Alphonse D'Amato	New York	3.6
25 Rudy Boschwitz	Minnesota	3.6

Source: Computed by author from National Election Studies, 1978–1994.

Indeed, William Dickinson's (R-Ala.) retirement in 1992 was prompted by a series of alleged ethical violations; he made his critics look prophetic by converting approximately $55,104 in leftover campaign funds to personal use, including a lump-sum salary payment of $17,500 to his wife. Among the senators with the lowest levels of reputational capital, Joe Biden (D-Del.) has found it difficult to live down his false declaration of working-class roots made during his unsuccessful (and brief) presidential candidacy in 1987; and Dennis DeConcini (D-Ariz.) was one of the infamous "Keating Five" who improperly intervened with federal regulators to help the soon-to-be bankrupt Lincoln Savings and Loan Association. Is it at all surprising that the reputational capital of these legislators has suffered? The available information supports the

TABLE 4.3
Top Twenty-Five Representatives in Terms of Reputational Capital

Representative	State	Net Reputational Capital (%)
1 Jack Kingston	Georgia	51.4
2 Elliot Levitas	Georgia	34.4
3 James Jones	Oklahoma	32.1
4 David Evans	Indiana	29.7
5 Lee Hamilton	Indiana	28.8
6 Charles Stenholm	Texas	28.6
7 Charles Bennett	Florida	27.5
8 Gladys Spellman	Maryland	25.7
9 Peter Defazio	Oregon	25.7
10 Stewart McKinney	Connecticut	25.6
11 Jan Meyers	Kansas	24.7
12 Virginia Smith	Nebraska	23.9
13 Harold Johnson	California	23.7
14 Jill Long	Indiana	23.1
15 Charles Pashayan	California	22.7
16 F. J. Sensenbrenner	Wisconsin	22.2
17 Bruce Morrison	Connecticut	21.5
18 Marilyn Lloyd	Tennessee	21.3
19 Timothy Penny	Minnesota	21.0
20 Clarence Long	Maryland	20.5
21 J.J. Pickle	Texas	20.4
22 Dante Fascell	Florida	20.4
23 Tom Railsback	Illinois	20.0
24 David Satterfield	Virginia	19.5
25 Parren Mitchell	Maryland	19.3

Source: Computed by author from National Election Studies, 1978–1994.

rankings of senators and representatives based upon my measurement of reputational capital, and further strengthens claims to the validity of the measure.

Is it possible that such perceptions (likes/dislikes) of trustworthiness are unrelated to reputations, but merely represent election-time theatrics? Specifically, if voter characterizations of legislators are purely a response to electioneering, with voters merely mimicking campaign messages, we might expect the six-year term of senators to introduce a cycle — an electoral cycle — where constituent perceptions vary across a senator's term of office. Such a cycle might take shape in the following manner. Opportunistic senators running for reelection might intensify their contacts with voters to increase perceptions of trustworthiness;

TABLE 4.4
Lowest Twenty-Five Representatives in Terms of Reputational Capital

Representative	State	Net Reputational Capital (%)
1 Calvin Dooley	California	− 28.2
2 Charles Grassley	Iowa	− 16.9
3 David Bonior	Michigan	− 12.1
4 James Moran	Virginia	− 9.4
5 Robert Badham	California	− 5.7
6 John Doolittle	California	− 4.9
7 Richard Baker	Louisiana	− 4.9
8 Jerry Lewis	California	− 3.6
9 Beryl Anthony	Arkansas	− 3.2
10 Edward Roybal	California	− 3.1
11 Martin Sabo	Minnesota	− 2.7
12 James Weaver	Oregon	− 2.3
13 William Dickinson	Alabama	− 2.0
14 Charles Wilson	Texas	− 1.9
15 John Miller	Washington	− 1.8
16 Thomas Ashley	Ohio	− 1.6
17 Dan Rostenkowski	Illinois	− 1.2
18 Donald Payne	New Jersey	− .6
19 Glenn Browder	Alabama	− .5
20 Bill Zeliff	New Hampshire	− .4
21 James Barcia	Michigan	− .1
22 Lionel VanDeerlin	California	− .02
23 Joseph Kennedy	Massachusetts	− .02
24 Craig Thomas	Wyoming	.0
25 William Gray	Pennsylvania	.0

Source: Computed by author from National Election Studies, 1978–1994.

other senators, without a pending reelection contest, would refrain from such increased contact, preferring to wait until the appropriate time — that being when their senate seat is up for reelection. If the attention that politicians shower upon their constituents is merely a response to elections, then legislators who are not facing an election should be perceived less in terms of trust than those facing an election. Evidence of an electoral cycle to these images would suggest that these images are electorally driven and engineered.

The images of senators reveal no evidence of an electoral cycle. In table 4.5 I report the likes/dislikes for senators at different stages in their terms: freshmen, and senators completing the second, fourth, and final year in their six-year term. There is no evidence that the images of

TABLE 4.5
Images and the Electoral Cycle: Senators in 1990

Content of Likes/ Dislikes[a]	Freshman Senators		Senators Reelected in 1988		Senators Reelected in 1984		Senators Reelected in 1986	
	Likes	Dislikes	Likes	Dislikes	Likes	Dislikes	Likes	Dislikes
	(%)		(%)		(%)		(%)	
Leadership	3	3	3	5	2	4	3	5
Experience	17	5	16	3	19	2	18	2
Constituency Service	18	9	17	10	18	12	19	11
Trust	13	17	15	16	13	14	13	16
Personal Characteristics	7	3	10	4	9	5	9	4
Party	5	15	4	15	4	15	3	13
Ideology	7	10	9	15	7	13	8	16
Domestic Issues	17	21	12	15	14	16	13	16
Foreign Policy Issues	2	4	2	4	2	4	2	4
Group Support	7	7	7	5	5	5	5	5
Miscellaneous	3	5	5	9	6	8	5	8
Cumulative Percent	99	99	100	101	99	98	98	100
N =	684	204	3,777	1,340	3,239	1,112	3,392	1,121

Source: Compiled by author from National Election Studies, Senate Elections in Context 1988–1990 Pooled File.
[a]Table entries show the percentage of all responses that fall into each category.

senators differ according to stages in the senate term: in 1990, freshmen senators were perceived in about the same way as more senior senators, and senators running for reelection were viewed no differently than those without a pressing reelection. The six-year senate term would seem an appropriate place to find electorally driven reputations, but there is no evidence of that fact. In sum, the content, construct, face, and predictive validity of the measurement of reputational capital reduces the possibility that the observed relationships uncovered in this analysis are largely derivative of problems of measurement.

CONCLUSION

This inquiry is eclectic in its analytic approach. Statistical procedures include marginals, graphs, tabular representations, correlation coefficients, analyses of variance and covariance, and logit regressions. Whenever possible I have emphasized simplicity in the analysis, and let the questions under examination, and the fragile nature of the data, dictate the sophistication of the statistical procedures. I beg the reader's indulgence.

CHAPTER 5

Constraining Opportunism through Self-Policing

IN THIS CHAPTER, I explore a critical prediction of the model: reputational capital deters opportunism. As noted earlier, reputational capital describes the sunk investments politicians make in their *reputations for trustworthiness and dutiful service; political opportunism is defined as devious self-interest of an unethical or quasi-ethical nature.* To many cynics, it seems that in the normal course of "doing business" politicians always find a way to extract some preferential treatment for themselves that is, at best, quasi-ethical in nature. But the greater public exposure given to the dealings of public officials through ethics codes and disclosure requirements probably make politicians more eager to help those less in the public spotlight, like friends and relatives. For instance, Dan Burton (R-Ind.) has been accused of pressuring executive branch officials into making concessions for a campaign contributor who ran a medical school in the Caribbean. Or consider Majority Whip Tom DeLay (R-Tex.), who circulated a "Dear Colleague" letter to Republican House members in the 104th Congress in support of one of his brother's foreign business clients. Somewhat more brash, but still not overtly or explicitly illegal, are the notorious actions of Bud Shuster (R-Pa.), whose efforts helped a family friend secure a $3 million contract with the Department of Housing and Urban Development; Shuster then twice intervened with the executive branch to save the real estate developer some $350,000 in penalties owed for not paying workers "prevailing wages" on federal projects. The real estate developer he helped happened to be a partner in a car dealership with Shuster's two sons and one of the dealership's initial financial backers.[1]

Politicians also seem to have an uncanny knack for exploiting institutional privileges and personal prerogatives. For example, many senators (until recently) were not the least bit reluctant to let their bills at the Senate Restaurants fall delinquent. Between 1984 and 1991, more than 20 percent of the "tabs" of senators were left outstanding for more than sixty days; in total dollars, the outstanding debt ranged during this period from a low of $247,034 in 1987 to a high of $384,712 in 1990. Such modest sums of money might be easily excused as representing lapses in memory rather than conscience. Perhaps senators are too busy to give much attention to the minor inconvenience of paying a bill here

TABLE 5.1
Aging of Customer Accounts at Senate Restaurants

Year	Days of Outstanding Debts (%)				Total Dollars
	0–30	31–60	61–90	Over 90	
1984	72[a]	6	2	20	$251,976
1985	66	7	8	19	272,894
1986	62	9	5	24	357,370
1987	58	9	8	25	247,034
1988	60	8	6	26	355,474
1989	74	4	7	15	373,348
1990	69	7	9	15	384,712
1991	65	4	10	21	311,192
1992[b]	97	1	2	0	170,858
1993	94	1	3	2	188,287
1994	97	2	1	0	171,020
1995	87	9	3	1	123,847
1996	81	9	3	7	195,189

Source: U.S. General Accounting Office, Financial Audits of Senate Restaurants Revolving Fund for Fiscal Year 1984 to 1996.

[a]Percentage of accounts paid within that time period.

[b]Effective January 1, 1992, the Senate Committee on Rules and Administration authorized the Senate Restaurants to assess a 2 percent penalty to delinquent customer accounts for each 30-day period of delinquency.

or there, or other bills that senators receive are given a higher priority because they entail staff salaries or market transactions.

This seems like a reasonable argument, but a closer examination of the figures in table 5.1 reveals an unusual change in delinquent accounts after 1991: the percentage of accounts at the Senate Restaurants that are delinquent for sixty or more days declines from 31 percent to 2 percent in 1993; in fact after 1992, the percentage never exceeds 10 percent. In addition, the debt left outstanding also declines significantly after 1991. For example, in 1991 outstanding bills amounted to $311,192 but in 1992 the debt was $170,858. In fact, at no time since 1991 did the level of outstanding debt reach the levels attained prior to 1991.

So what happened in 1992? In that year, the Senate Committee on Rules and Administration levied a 2 percent penalty on all delinquent accounts for each thirty-day period. If delinquent accounts were merely a cost of the job, senators might ignore this rather trifling penalty; however, if the Senate Restaurants' bill-collection procedures were the object of devious exploitation, this type of penalty should reduce opportunism to a significant degree. Indeed, after 1992 delinquent accounts almost disappear as 80–97 percent of the restaurant bills are paid within thirty

TABLE 5.2
Aging of Customer Accounts at House Restaurants

| Year | Days of Outstanding Debts (%) | | | | Total Dollars |
	0–30	31–60	61–90	Over 90	
1984	75[a]	3	5	17	$319,044
1985	18	42	8	32	316,703
1989	22	38	16	24	826,035

Source: U.S. General Accounting Office, *Financial Audit of House Restaurant Revolving Fund for 1989 and 1985, and Service America Corporation's 1988 Operation of the House Restaurant System.*
[a]Percentage of accounts paid within that time period.

days! The House of Representatives, in contrast, has no such penalty and, not surprisingly, delinquency shows little evidence of dissipating. In fact, although the evidence is sparse, the number of dollars involved may actually be increasing along with levels of delinquency (table 5.2). It is not the sums of money that are important here. What is important is that legislators would take full advantage of their positions to engage in practices that resulted in such minor economic gain! Just a small penalty was sufficient to halt the practice in the Senate.

Some acts of opportunism seem to have become acceptable political practice. For example, presidential appointment of judges to posts with lifetime tenure is an area where opportunism might arise, especially as presidents near the end of their first term of office. Admittedly, presidents should resist taking advantage of their power to appoint judges (with senate approval) until the end of their *final* (second) term since only then are they truly in their last period of officeholding; however, the uncertainty of most reelections—only Ronald Reagan and William Clinton have been reelected since 1964—probably leads most presidents to seize the opportunity to leave their imprint on federal laws at the first opportunity—in their first term. The appointment of federal judges enables presidents to leave a legacy that incorporates their economic, social, and ideological views—an imprint on government that may far surpass changes in public policy induced through electoral turnover. Thus, we might expect opportunistic presidents to make more lifetime judicial appointments in the penultimate or final year of their first term.

In figure 5.1 I display the percentage of (total) lifetime judicial appointments made each year of a president's four-year term of office. By and large, the graph reveals the hypothesized pattern: Peaks in appointment percentages occur in the penultimate year of many presidents'

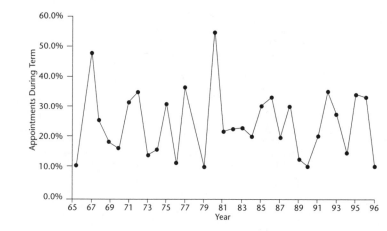

Figure 5.1 Lifetime Judicial Appointments. *Source*: Compiled by author from *The Weekly Compilation of Presidential Documents, 1965–1996*.

terms of office (e.g., Nixon, 1971; Carter, 1979; Bush, 1991), or in their final year (i.e., Nixon, 1974; Ford, 1976; Reagan, 1984). The notable exceptions to this pattern are: Reagan's second term (1985–1988), where the percentage of appointments in the penultimate year (31.1%), while considerable, were just a few percentages below the level in 1985 (34.9%), and the Johnson presidency, where lifetime judicial appointments peaked in 1966 rather than 1967 or 1968. Are presidents exploiting last-period conditions? The evidence seems quite suggestive of this possibility.

It might be argued that merely bringing to light episodes of opportunism in defaulting on restaurant bills, or making last-period lifetime appointments, is sufficient to deter questionable conduct. This is certainly a reasonable and defensible contention. Monitoring might be effective when public attention is strongly focused because of the widespread visibility of a political scandal (e.g., House bank scandal). Such conditions elevate levels of public concern, thereby increasing the incentives for monitoring the behavior of politicians, as well as reducing some of the costs involved in acquiring information about ethical conduct. Although publicity is not easy to manufacture, occasionally questions of ethical conduct gain public notice through congressional hearings. Despite the behind-the-scenes resistance of legislators, congressional hearings exploring the ethical and legal proprieties of government officials are rather probing. But do citizens pay much attention to these revelations of wrongdoing? Apparently not, at least in recent years. While the Iran-Contra Affair caught the attention of 72 percent of the respondents

TABLE 5.3
Public Attention to Major Congressional Hearings

| | | Percentage of Respondents Following Hearings | | |
Subject of Hearings	Year	Very closely	Fairly closely	Total
Iran-Contra Affair	1987	33	39	72
U.S. Persian Gulf Policy	1991	22	36	58
Federal Raid on Waco	1995	18	35	53
Whitewater Investigation	1995	11	26	37
FBI Siege at Ruby Ridge	1995	11	26	37
Campaign Contributions	1997	10	28	38

Source: *Congressional Quarterly*, November 1, 1997, 2657.

interviewed in 1987 (followed the hearings either "very closely" or "fairly closely"), a decade later, only 38 percent (1997) expressed a similar level of interest in the congressional hearings on campaign contributions (table 5.3). In fact, since the hearings on the Iran-Contra Affair, interest in congressional hearings has waned. If the public cares little about monitoring the actions of politicians, why should politicians worry about their opportunistic dealings being uncovered, or if uncovered, leaving an indelible mark on the voter's conscience?

OPPORTUNISM IN CONGRESS

Not everyone would agree with the premise that reputational capital reduces opportunism:

[E]conomists assume politicians are "experience" goods since quality (whether a politician delivers what he promises voters) can only be evaluated through experience post-election and that this quality is guaranteed by the threatened removal from office . . . [P]oliticians could make sunk investments (e.g., political brand name) that they earn some competitive return on in each subsequent period. If the present value of this premium is greater than the gain to cheating the politician will not cheat. However, in the last period it will always pay for him to cheat. If voters know the politician is in his last period, they would not want to elect him, and thus he would cheat in the next to last period, and the whole process unravels. . . . [S]unk investments cannot eliminate opportunistic behavior in the last period when a politician has decided to retire and thus knows with certainty that he will no longer face reelection. (Lott 1987, 169–170)

While John Lott believes that reputational goodwill cannot constrain opportunism, Joseph Kalt and Mark Zupan (1990) go so far as to suggest that reputational capital actually increases opportunism. They contend that legislators with good brand names spend their capital on shirking. Brand-name capital cushions the loss of voter support resulting from revelations of shirking:

> Just as a firm's brand-name capital might allow that firm's products to be trusted and less carefully inspected by customers, so brand-name capital could be expected to reduce the incremental support loss of a senator's shirking. The more brand-name capital a senator has built up with constituents, the fewer disgruntled constituents are created by incremental shirking; at the margin, the existence of a brand name leads constituents to discount their perceptions of shirking, less support is lost. (Kalt and Zupan 1990, 119)

In the following pages I examine whether reputational capital (or goodwill) constrains various examples of unethical or quasi-unethical behavior in Congress, and how revelations of questionable conduct affect such capital.

Shirking

While there are numerous ways in which opportunism can emerge in the U.S. Congress, this analysis focuses on three examples. First, legislators may "shirk" their responsibilities in the production of public policy. "Shirking" is normally revealed when a rational individual fails to give a full effort in executing tasks. For many economists, it amounts to simply trading "work" for "leisure." As applied to politics and politicians, shirking results from slack in legislative institutions (e.g., lack of monitoring), thereby allowing members considerable leeway in their Washington behavior. Thus, failure to provide a full effort in the execution of one's duties is a description of shirking that fits well into the analysis of faithful agents since it calls attention to the expectation that representatives are to execute their responsibilities to the fullest extent possible. This form of shirking is measured in terms of levels of voting participation ("participatory shirking") by House incumbents between 1977 and 1994. Voters expect their representatives to faithfully participate in all deliberative actions and policy decisions; to do otherwise can be construed as shirking. Given obstacles to effective monitoring, opportunistic legislators should vote less frequently. On the other hand, reputable legislators (those with high levels of reputational capital) will eschew such shirking and devoutly attend to their legislative duties, like voting on the House floor.

Last-Period Problems

Second, opportunism may occur as legislators encounter last-period problems. Legislators planning to leave, or retire from, congressional service have an incentive to take advantage of their offices since they no longer face discipline at the hands of voters. As noted earlier, there is considerable disagreement among scholars as to the importance or even the existence of last-period problems (see Lott 1987, 1990; Lott and Davis 1992; Zupan 1990; Kalt and Zupan 1990; Vanbeek 1991; Parker 1996). Most of the studies dealing with last-period problems have examined changes in roll-call voting in the last term of officeholding, but few have explored other possible expressions of opportunistic dealings. One obvious area for opportunism is lame-duck travel—that is, foreign travel taken by exiting (voluntarily) or retiring members of Congress.

Despite existing restrictions, foreign travel is difficult to police not only because loopholes exist in the rules, but also because foreign travel involves moral hazards. For example, who can determine what a legislator is observing and recording on these trips? Since voters cannot observe all the elements of the legislator's behavior, they cannot tell if he or she has violated representational responsibilities. As a consequence, voters have little alternative but to accept the explanations given by their legislator, or incur very high monitoring costs.

Can the fear of losing brand-name capital prevent last-period problems from emerging? The model of reputational control implies that one reason legislators eschew opportunism is because of the potential loss in reputational goodwill that might occur if those transgressions became public. Most criticisms of the sunk-investment approach question whether such a mechanism can eliminate opportunistic behavior *in the last period*—when a politician has decided to leave office and thus knows with certainty that he or she will no longer face the threat of reelection (see, for example, Lott 1987 and 1990).[2] A politician can then milk his or her reputation without fear that voters will exact a price for such behavior the next time around. However, if politicians can "sell" their reputations for nonopportunistic dealings, then last-period problems dissipate. If sunk investments yield a premium in terms of post-elective employment as well as electoral safety, then their capacity to constrain unethical behavior is significantly enhanced. Sunk investments, alone, may not be sufficient to deter some forms of opportunism, but in conjunction with premiums for trustworthiness, they have a greater potential for success.

Lame-duck travel is a good place to look for expressions of legislator opportunism because shirking can be expected to focus on activities that are difficult to police and for which there are poor substitutes off the job (Kalt and Zupan 1984, 283). Distinguishing lame-duck travel from the execution of overseas, congressional fact-finding missions is no easy task that is made even more trying by the moral hazard problem discussed earlier. Simply put, there is no unobtrusive way to differentiate legislators consuming lame-duck travel from those who travel overseas in their last term of office in the faithful execution of their legislative duties. Who will admit to frivolous, unethical behavior? I approach this question of lame-duck travel by examining the changes in the days of foreign travel between the penultimate and last term of officeholding for House members who exited office voluntarily; foreign travel is recorded for the House members exiting between the years of 1978 and 1992.[3] The attraction of lame-duck travel should lead exiting legislators to *increase* the number of days of foreign travel they consume prior to departing the House of Representatives, but faithful agents should travel less in the last period as their legislative responsibilities wind down. Such behavior helps to preserve the reputational capital of faithful agents.

Private Gain

As mentioned earlier in this chapter, legislators may behave opportunistically by exploiting institutional prerogatives for private gain. There have been a variety of such episodes, but the most sensational may be Dan Rostenkowski (D-Ill.), who sold postage stamps back to the House Post Office, and pocketed the cash; other audacious examples could be described but I need not belabor the obvious point.[4] The Rostenkowski case was unusual in that his actions were not merely unethical but also highly illegal. Nonetheless, there are numerous ways in which legislators can exploit their institutional positions opportunistically rather than illegally, and still obtain monetary gain. Two ways examined in this chapter are through the collection of honoraria and the kiting of checks at the House bank. Both of these avenues of opportunistic behavior are now closed; again, ex post reactions for controlling opportunism.

Although the practice has now been eliminated, at an earlier point in time legislators could collect considerable amounts of money by merely giving a speech to, or discussing issues with, individuals and groups with an interest in government policy. Prior to elimination, there were legal limits on the amount of money that legislators were allowed to keep from earned honoraria: 30 percent of a representative's salary and 40 percent of a senator's salary. There were no limits, however, to the amount earned, only the amount retained. Money in excess of these limits was required to be contributed to charity. Despite this charitable aspect to the raising of honoraria dollars, financial benefits still accrued since legislators could count these sums as income for purposes of increasing tax deductions. Although any restraint on the income earned through honoraria might constrain this quasi-legal activity, many senators and representatives still earned honoraria way beyond the stipulated limit.

I have measured this form of opportunism as simply the total amount of honoraria (dollars) collected by House and Senate members in my analysis during the years 1989 and 1990. Measurements of reputational capital are recorded both before and after revelations of honoraria earnings. By comparing legislators' reputational capital *prior* to public revelations, with the level of capital *after* that measurement, we can test for the impact of public awareness of this quasi-ethical behavior on changes in reputational capital. Unfortunately, measurements of the reputational capital of senators could only be obtained after revelations of their honoraria earnings; hence, the relationship between the reputational capital of senators and the raising of honoraria is probably less reliable.

Check kiting is another example of how members behave unethically or opportunistically in exploiting prerogatives of the office. Check kiting is commonly defined as the writing of one check while knowing that there are insufficient funds in the account drawn upon, and then attempting to cover the first check with a second check drawn on another account with insufficient funds. This appears to aptly describe the situation that led to the demise of the House bank. The House bank had three distinct advantages for legislators intent upon gaining from a check-kiting scheme. First, representatives received an unusual "grace period" before they had to "make good" on a "bad" check. The normal practice was to accept rather than reject checks drawn by legislators with insufficient funds; legislators were contacted later and asked to make up the deficits. Second, legislators were aware that a bad check would never be sent back through channels without them first being informed and given a chance to cover the check's deficit. Finally, by honoring thousands of checks that most commercial banks would have returned due to insufficient funds, the House bank permitted legislators to engage in conduct that would have been impossible, and possibly illegal, for the general public.

On the surface, the House bank seems a rather innocent endeavor: it was a depository where members could keep their salaries and money in checking accounts. Much like a commercial bank, the House bank took deposits, issued check books, cashed checks, and issued monthly statements of deposits and debits. Unlike a commercial bank, however, the House bank did not pay interest on deposits, make interest-bearing loans, or invest bank assets for profit. One of the crucial distinctions between commercial banks and the House bank is that the latter had a far more generous policy of handling bad checks than did commercial banks.

Opportunistic legislators who wrote checks for more money than they had in their accounts had little to worry about since the House bank would almost always honor them and delay collecting the debt. This is not how commercial banks handle overdrafts. Unless the individual who wrote the check has overdraft protection, commercial banks normally "bounce" such checks. That is, the overdraft checks are returned to the person to whom they were written, and the check writer is then charged a fee. If the account holder has overdraft protection, the bank issues a loan to cover the check and charges the check writer interest on the loan; overdraft protection at a commercial bank is usually a line of credit with a rather steep short-term interest rate. What eventually erupted into a full-blown scandal was not that the House bank refused to bounce checks, but rather that they paid the check and delayed charging the legislator until his or her account contained sufficient funds to cover the overdrafts. This procedure, in essence, rewarded legislators with interest-free loans that were considerable in size; Carl Perkins (D-Ky.) and Stephen Solarz (D.-N.Y.), for example, bounced over $500,000 of worthless checks during a three-year period.

The absence of monitoring procedures at the House bank made it an attractive place for opportunistic dealings. Members never suspected that their actions would come to light, especially in an institutionally established and patronage-run organization. Opportunism thrives in such secretive situations, but reputational capital can be expected to deter check kiting even under such propitious conditions. Therefore, I expect a negative relationship between levels of reputational capital and the number of checks kited at the House bank. I have measured reputational capital prior to 1990, when the scandal began to emerge, because I do not want the measurement of reputational capital to be confounded by investigations at the House bank, nor the check-kiting behavior of legislators.

Can Reputational Capital Deter Acts of Opportunism?

Two conditions sustain self-policing: "First, self-enforcing agreements are not feasible if the sequence of occasions for transactions has a definite last element. Although termination is certain to occur sooner or later, when this happens must be uncertain to sustain a self-enforcing agreement. Second, for a given sequence of gains, the expected horizon must be long enough or there can be no self-enforcing agreement.

Equivalently, the longer is the expected horizon, the greater is the return to the parties from adhering to the terms of the agreement" (Telser 1980, 44). While it may not seem obvious, these two conditions conducive to self-policing characterize Congress: termination through election, although improbable, remains uncertain (Mann 1978), and the expected career horizon of most legislators is exceedingly long (Polsby 1968).

The premium of post-elective employment as an incentive to discourage opportunistic behavior extends further the career horizons of legislators, thereby reducing the likelihood that last-period conditions will be exploited. "A sequence has no last term if there is always a positive probability of continuing. As long as this is true, anyone who violates the terms at one time incurs the risk of losses in the future. Therefore, there is no certainty of gain from a violation of the agreement on any transaction because there is always a positive probability of continuing to another transaction" (Telser 1980, 29). Exiting legislators may not have to face an electorate again, but they may have to face employers. A politician's last term of office may not actually represent his or her "last period" in any meaningful sense of the term, since so few legislators actually "retire" when they exit Congress.

While I rely upon a quasi-experimental analysis for determining whether reputational capital is capable of constraining opportunism, some preliminary evidence supports this claim. For instance, table 5.4 reports the zero-order correlations between previously described acts of opportunism and reputational capital. The simplicity of the analysis notwithstanding, the conclusion is obvious: Reputational capital has a consistently significant, but admittedly modest, effect in constraining acts of opportunism. For instance, of the eighteen years of voting attendance, reputational capital increased voting participation by a significant amount in one-half of them (level of significance $\leq .05$); and in three additional time periods (i.e., 1981, 1990, and 1993) the magnitude of the correlations approached a statistically significant relationship as defined here. Equally relevant is the *consistency in the direction* of the correlation coefficients. In every instance, reputational capital is positively related to voting participation scores. Self-policing seems to surface here: Faithful agents shirk their responsibilities for attending floor votes significantly less than the untrustworthy, although the magnitude of the relationships is not earth-shattering.

Reputational capital seems about as effective in curtailing abuses of congressional privileges, such as the collection of honoraria (House, $r = -.19$; Senate, $r = -.15$) and the kiting of checks at the House bank ($r = -.18$). Reputational capital is associated with lower levels of honoraria income, and check kiting, although the latter relationship

TABLE 5.4
Does a Reputation as a Faithful Agent Deter Acts of Opportunism?
(Pearson Correlation with Reputation as a Faithful Agent)

Activity	Number of Cases	Pearson Correlation	Significance Level[a]
House: Honoraria collected in 1989 and 1990 (natural logarithms)[b]	81	−.19	.041*
Senate: Honoraria collected in 1989 and 1990 (natural logarithms)	88	−.15	.087
Kiting checks at House Bank[b]	81	−.18	.059*
Voting Participation 1977	109	.09	.170
Voting Participation 1978	109	.22	.009*
Voting Participation 1979	130	.10	.211
Voting Participation 1980	129	.27	.001*
Voting Participation 1981	137	.12	.073
Voting Participation 1982	137	.05	.285
Voting Participation 1983	141	.17	.019*
Voting Participation 1984	140	.15	.034*
Voting Participation 1985	145	.19	.012*
Voting Participation 1986	145	.02	.402
Voting Participation 1987	143	.18	.014*
Voting Participation 1988	140	.25	.001*
Voting Participation 1989	143	.16	.029*
Voting Participation 1990	143	.13	.067
Voting Participation 1991	138	.04	.320
Voting Participation 1992	138	.14	.045*
Voting Participation 1993	111	.13	.087
Voting Participation 1994	111	.05	.317

[a]One-tailed significance test.
[b]Reputational capital is calculated prior to 1989.
*Significant at .05 level.

falls slightly below what I have regarded as an appropriate level of statistical significance (i.e., .05 level). Again, the signs of the relationships are in the predicted (negative) direction. Reputational capital, however, has almost no significant effect on the honoraria earnings of senators (level of significance = .09), as anticipated. But is reputational capital an effective constraint on last-period behavior which is immune from electoral control?

The impact of reputational capital in constraining last-period problems is best demonstrated through the quasi-experimental analysis shown in tables 5.5 and 5.6. In table 5.5, the results of applying an analysis of

TABLE 5.5
The Impact of Net Reputational Capital on Lame-Duck Foreign Travel

Source of Variation	Sum of Squares	DF	Mean Square	F	Significance[a] of F
1. Covariate: Days of foreign travel in the penultimate term[b]	7209.314	1	7209.314	75.402	.000
2. Main Effect: Net reputational capital (prior to exit)[b]	1257.802	3	419.267	4.385	.003
Explained	8467.116	4	2116.779	22.139	.000
Residual	7170.872	75	95.612		
Total	15637.988	79	197.949		
Number of cases = 80					

[a]One-tailed test of statistical significance.
[b]Net reputational capital has been classified into four categories:
1 = −16.91 to 3.84
2 = 4.67 to 8.58
3 = 9.52 to 16.65
4 = 17.80 to 32.07

covariance design to the question are shown. In this quasi-experimental design, the effects of foreign travel in the penultimate term are first removed.[5] This enables us to isolate the effects of reputational capital in reducing lame-duck travel by "correcting for" the influence of extraneous variation before the effects of reputational capital are assessed. This application is widely used in experimental and quasi-experimental research to eliminate variation in the dependent variable that cannot be controlled through experimental manipulations. In addition, social science methodologists argue that this method is preferable to the use of change scores (i.e., changes of days of foreign travel between the last and penultimate terms of officeholding) in analyzing over-time changes in behavior (Markus 1979).

Foreign travel in the last period is strongly related to reputational capital (table 5.5); such capital diminishes legislator demand for lame-duck travel. The importance of reputational capital can be seen in table 5.6, where I have subjected these results to a Multiple Classification Analysis. Net reputational capital explains 11.6 percent of the variation in lame-duck travel (eta = .34; eta^2 = 11.6), and after adjusting for the effects of travel in the penultimate term, lame-duck travel declines in

Table 5.6
Multiple Classification Analysis of the Impact of Net Reputational Capital on
Lame-Duck Foreign Travel

Net Reputational Capital	N	Unadjusted Category Effects	Adjusted Category Effects
−16.91–3.84	20	8.09	6.67
4.67–8.58	20	−3.71	−3.19
9.52–16.65	25	−2.11	−.87
17.80–32.07	15	−2.31	−3.19

Statistics:
  Eta = .34
  Beta = .28
  Multiple R = .736
  Multiple R^2 = .541
  Grand Mean = 8.11

each category of (increased) reputational capital (see "adjusted category effects"). The most faithful travel about three days less in their last term of office relative to the mean level for all exiting members (excluding those losing election), and about ten days less than the least faithful. In sum, there is evidence that reputational capital can constrain various forms of opportunism, and in particular, foreign travel in the last period.

Effects of Revelations of Opportunism on Reputational Capital

Faithful agents derive some external benefit from public revelations of opportunistic behavior, such as feelings of righteousness, notoriety, and the like, but perhaps the most important is that it enhances the value of dutiful conduct and trustworthiness. Voters are politely reminded by such revelations that they can be deceived quite easily in a world where information is scarce, complex, and asymmetric; hence, a legislator's faithfulness takes on added value. The same dynamics appear to operate in the market:

> Learning that it paid for the firm to commit fraud represents an external benefit, not a cost, because the detection of the fraud has informed the customers that the probability of being defrauded was higher than they had realized. The external benefit is not produced by the fraud itself but, rather, by the information that at least one firm

considered fraud to be profitable. In fact, the sooner the information about the fraud is communicated, the shorter the period of time that consumers will be making purchases with less quality assurance then they would have purchased had they had the additional information. (Karpoff and Lott 1993, 762)

Here we examine the second part of the first hypothesis (see chapter 4) — namely, that signs of opportunism on the part of legislators diminish the latter's reputational goodwill. I test this proposition by examining the impact that public release of information about the honoraria earnings of House incumbents had on their subsequent levels of reputational capital. If reputations represent sunk investments, exposing the pursuit of personal quasi-ethical gains should result in losses in reputational capital, especially since the public is apprehensive about the taking of honoraria (chapter 1). Honoraria earnings are measured as the total number of dollars received in 1989 and 1990.

This section of the analysis also employs a quasi-experimental design by measuring reputational capital before and after the release of public information about the honoraria collected by House incumbents in 1989 and 1990. I have had to make some small but necessary adjustments to the prevailing research design to create before and after measurements of reputational capital for this part of the analysis. Specifically, before and after measurements of reputational capital are based upon those legislators with district samples greater than or equal to *twenty* rather than *twenty-nine*, as has been the rule throughout the analysis. This was necessary because of the stringent requirements placed on the legislators selected for this quasi-experimental analysis — namely, that they have continuously served in Congress between 1989 and 1994 and have had sufficient district measurements of faithfulness taken both *before* and *after* the 1989–1990 period (at least twenty respondents) to qualify for analysis. This unfortunately reduces our initial sample of 211 to a mere 26 legislators. (The reader should be reminded that the small sample size will bias the analysis *against* uncovering a statistically significant relationship.)

Reputational capital is measured at two time points. Time $t + 1$ corresponds to the measurement of reputational capital after the release of information about honoraria earnings, and reflects the pooling of the 1992 and 1994 National Election Studies' surveys. Time t corresponds to the measurement of reputational capital prior to the release of this information, and represents the pooling of National Election Studies' surveys between 1978 and 1988. A preliminary analysis reveals a strong negative correlation between changes in reputational capital between the two time periods and total honoraria earnings ($r = -.45$). Reputa-

TABLE 5.7
The Impact of Public Revelation of Honoraria Earnings on Net Reputational
Capital in 1992–1994

Source of Variation	Sum of Squares	DF	Mean Square	F	Significance[a]
1. Covariate: Net reputational capital, 1978–1988	5.645	1	5.645	.055	.408
2. Main Effect: Total honoraria earnings, 1989–1990[b]	264.605	1	264.605	2.555	.060
Explained	270.250	2	135.125	1.305	.145
Residual	2382.089	23	103.569		
Total	2652.339	25	106.094		
Number of cases = 26					

[a]One-tailed test of statistical significance.
[b]Honoraria earnings are classified into two categories:
   1 = 0–$20,750
   2 = $34,000–$318,214

tional capital declined significantly for House members who reported
the largest honoraria incomes. The problems with using such "change
scores" that I noted in the previous section are relevant in analyzing the
effects of honoraria earnings on reputational capital. So, as I have done
in the analysis of lame-duck travel, I address this question through an
analysis of covariance.

In table 5.7, the results of applying an analysis of covariance design
to this question are shown. To remove the effects that prior levels of
reputational capital (1978–1988) might have on levels of capital in
1992 and 1994, the former (covariate) was entered first into the analysis, and then the effects of honoraria earnings examined. Thus, variation in the dependent variable (i.e., reputational capital) due to the
covariate is removed before the effects of honoraria earnings are allowed to operate. It is clear from table 5.7 that the effect of revelations
of honoraria earnings on reputational capital approaches a statistically
significant level (significance level $\leq$ .06), and given the small sample
size, statistical significance of this magnitude is no easy task. In sum,
revelations of the high honoraria earnings of House incumbents appear
to reduce their reputational capital among their constituents.

While it would be difficult to precisely gauge the effects of such revelations, especially given the fragile nature of the data, the figures in
table 5.8 suggest that revelations of high honoraria earnings cost legisla-

TABLE 5.8
Multiple Classification Analysis of the Impact of Public Revelation of
Honoraria Earnings on Net Reputational Capital in 1992–1994

Total Honoraria, 1989–1990	N	Unadjusted Category Effects	Adjusted Category Effects
None–$20,750	12	3.21	4.03
$34,000–$318,214	14	−2.75	−3.45

Statistics:
  Eta = .29
  Beta = .37
  Multiple R = .319
  Multiple R^2 = .102
  Grand Mean = 8.69

tors about 7.5 percent in reputational goodwill relative to the level of reputational capital obtained by those who were reported as having lower honoraria incomes. In the market, public awareness of corporate error, as exhibited by product recalls, airline crashes, deceptive advertising, and fraud, result in the loss of reputational capital (see Jarrell and Peltzman 1985; Karpoff and Lott 1993; Rubin et al. 1988; Mitchell and Maloney 1989; Mitchell 1989). The reputational capital of legislators, likewise, rises and falls with public revelations of their wrongdoings.

CONCLUSION

It might seem that control of opportunism and unethical behavior is within our grasp, given the effectiveness of reputational capital in reducing a difficult last-period problem (i.e., lame-duck travel), and the consistent negative correlations between acts of opportunism (e.g., check kiting) and reputational capital. The solution seems quite simple: encourage legislators to invest heavily in their reputations as faithful agents; the greater the "capital" invested, the less attractive unethical behavior looks. But encouraging legislators to undertake these sunk costs may be more difficult than it might appear.

If reputational capital provides no assurance of job security, an important incentive for making *large* sunk investments is lost. Clearly, voters favor such a reputation (trustworthiness), and employers find faithful agents equally valuable. Still, voters are willing to accept less, and many employers are unwilling or unable to provide a sufficient number of post-elective employment opportunities to satisfy the demands of faithful agents. Legislators can gain reelection without incurring the costs associated with ethical conduct, and the lack of a large supply of good jobs leads many members of Congress to discount the value of future employment. Under such conditions, rational behavior should lead many legislators to minimize their investments in reputational capital because the costs outweigh the gains. This impedes the ability of reputational capital to constrain opportunism and unethical behavior. In the next chapter, I explore the extent to which a faithful-agent reputation pays off in terms of job security — the premium paid trustworthy legislators.

Reputational Capital and Job Security; or, If Trustworthy Legislators Are at a Premium, Are They Paid One?

IN THE LAST CHAPTER evidence was presented suggesting that reputational capital has the capacity to constrain unethical and quasi-ethical conduct in Congress, and that losses in capital can occur when information about such behavior becomes public. Fear of losing reputational capital appears to be a viable incentive for constraining opportunism, but for reputational controls to be truly effective, there also must be significant payoffs to faithful behavior. The second hypothesis suggests that trustworthy legislators earn premiums for their propriety. Reelection is only one of the premiums awarded faithful agents; attractive post-elective employment is the other. Legislators want to maintain an earnings stream, so they consider not only continuing their legislative careers but also the possibility that those careers might come to a conclusion. Aside from endearing legislators to their constituents, a reputation as a faithful agent signals potential employers that the legislator is a good risk for employment, especially where shirking is difficult or costly to detect. In this chapter, the proposition that a reputation as a faithful agent engenders electoral support and attractive post-elective employment for the electorally unsuccessful is examined.

Four points are made in this section of the inquiry. First, perceptions of trustworthiness influence voting in House elections even when the impact of other major electoral forces are considered, but their effects are far more problematic in Senate contests. Second, reputational capital, while electorally beneficial, has to compete with other reputational signals that are even more influential in voter decisions (e.g., party identification). Third, reputational goodwill sustains career longevity and enhances prospects for attractive post-elective employment, *if legislators lose reelection, or election to higher office.* Finally, the effectiveness of elections as ex post mechanisms for punishing opportunism and corruption may be exaggerated.

There are few studies of the effects of reputational trust on congressional elections (see, for instance, Parker 1989; Mondak 1995; McCurley and Mondak 1995). One attempt to address this lacunae is the ambitious work of Jeffery Mondak (1995; McCurley and Mondak 1995), who studied the effects of "integrity" on House elections. The differences between his research approach to this question and that used here are rather fundamental. Perhaps the most basic is that Mondak based his estimates of legislator integrity on the accounts of political observers and pundits, editorialized in biographical accounts, while this analysis defines trustworthiness in terms of publicly held conceptions (i.e., data derived from constituent opinions and perceptions). Arguably, the latter operationalization better approximates the *public nature* of "reputations."

Mondak's data are derived from content analyses of written descriptions of House members who entered the House of Representatives between 1969 and 1981, and appearing in the 1972–94 volumes of the *Almanac of American Politics*. All words and phrases in these descriptions that broadly referenced "competence" and "integrity" were defined, and the resulting list of words and phrases were rated on two scales by undergraduate students at the University of Pittsburgh. Students were asked to evaluate each trait in terms of whether it was positive or negative, and whether the trait reflected competence or integrity; they assigned scores to each term on a 0 to 1 scale. A legislator's rating is the mean quality score for all terms and phrases used in the largely repetitive biographical descriptions in the *Almanac of American Politics*. For example, legislator integrity is represented by the mean quality score for all items that referenced integrity. Mondak concluded from his analyses that integrity—a variable conceptually similar to my definition of a faithful-agent reputation—influenced House elections.

While Mondak has taken precautions to ensure the reliability and validity of his measurements, his conclusions are open to question on several grounds. First, aside from bearing no obvious connection to constituency opinion, biographical sketches in the *Almanac of American Politics* fail to deal with many aspects of a legislator's reputation, such as constituent service. Since his analyses only probed two attitudes—integrity and competence—the effects of these two variables on electoral vote may be capturing some additional reputational effects, namely, the influence of other reputations (see table 3.1) not measured in the biographical sketches but nonetheless salient in voter opinion. Second, variables important in predicting voter choice (e.g., popularity of the incumbent) are absent from the explanatory equations. In light of these problems, we cannot dismiss the possibility that the results Mondak reports are due to inadequately specified equations (and variables) that ignore other factors that also influence House elections. Third, the relationship between trust and voting in Senate elections remains unexplored. If trust, or integrity, is important to electoral outcomes, does it also affect Senate as well as House elections?

This is not intended to assail the conclusions Mondak reaches, nor his novel methodology. My point is that the impact of trustworthiness, or integrity, on congressional elections is far from settled, and existing evidence is less than convincing. My analysis addresses some of the shortcomings in Mondak's approach: I use opinion data rather than students' ratings of legislator attributes; the equations for explaining voter choice in congressional elections include far more variables, thereby reducing specification problems; the analysis deals with voting in Senate as well as House elections; and the study entails an examination of the effects of other substitutes to a faithful-agent reputation on voting in congressional elections. Thus, my approach should supply a unique angle to the question of the role of reputational trust in congressional elections. In addition, my analysis of the role of trust in Senate elections offers an hypothesis that differs from conventional expectations. I expect trust will be less important to voting decisions in Senate elections because senators have even fewer incentives to build reputational capital than representatives do; hence, it plays a smaller role in their appeals for votes. Senators, like representatives, can promote less costly reputations, but unlike representatives, senators have considerably far less need of reputational goodwill to obtain attractive post-elective employment. Moreover, senators have a longer "repurchase" period with the six-year term. This encourages shirking since voter awareness is likely to decay over such a long time period (Figlio 2000). Thus, senators' trust, or lack thereof, is likely to be forgotten by voters.

In this segment of the analysis the electoral effects of the images and reputations of incumbents are examined. The independent variables analyzed here are common to most studies of voting in congressional elections. In addition, they can be viewed as reflecting the types of associations and perceptions that are the bases of legislators' reputations. That is, these attitudes can be viewed as products of the diffusion of reputational information and messages. The list of "predictors" is not intended to be exhaustive. They are introduced into the explanatory equations to assure that perceptions of trustworthiness are not merely capturing variation left unexplained because important variables have been excluded or ignored, and because they reflect the types of reputational information and messages that characterize competing reputations.

"Substitute" reputations, by providing electorally rewarding alternatives to a faithful-agent reputation, cheapen the value of the premium paid trustworthy politicians — namely, that portion of the premium that ensures electoral safety. If this premium is so eroded, the rationale un-derlying the establishment of a faithful-agent reputation is less compel-ling. It is too much, however, to expect trustworthiness to dominate electoral choice; substitute reputations, like partisan identification, seem certain to rival trust in the minds of many voters for a variety of rea-sons. Nonetheless, trustworthy legislators need to feel confident that their efforts to maintain their reputability will pay off to a significant degree. At the very least, they need to feel that voters regard trust-worthiness as an important legislator attribute when making electoral decisions. In short, a reputation for trustworthiness should be competi-tive with other legislator reputations.

Thus, the explanatory equations include variables that are at the same time important predictors of electoral behavior as well as the underpin-nings of reputations that serve as substitutes for a faithful-agent reputa-tion. If an electoral premium is paid trustworthy legislators, the rela-tionship between electoral choice and reputational trust should at least be significant despite the existence of alternative voting cues designed to persuade voters to take other things into consideration. The dependent variable in the first section of the analysis in this chapter is whether or not a respondent voted for the incumbent senator or representative (coded 1 if yes, and 0 otherwise). The findings are based on the Ameri-can National Election Studies 1991 Pooled Data Set.[1]

REPUTATIONS AND ELECTORAL BEHAVIOR

Reputational capital should have a significant impact on electoral sup-port even when consideration is given to the other forces that influence voter choice in congressional elections. Its effect is limited, however, to the extent that there are other more potent influences on congressional voting. Rational legislators consider not only their level of reputational capital but whether they might find some less costly way of inducing voter support. And substitute reputations do just that.

One substitute to a faithful-agent reputation is an ideological reputa-tion; ideology is also an important electoral force. Legislators can boast of their liberalism or conservatism, and point to salient roll-call deci-sions, in an effort to persuade voters that they are positioned at a cer-tain place along the ideological continuum—hopefully, the same ideo-logical position as voters. While issue voting is not the rule, the ideological preferences of voters can be incited in electoral politics, for example, Senate elections (Wright and Berkman 1986). Ideological rep-utations serve as substitutes for faithful-agent reputations because they bind politicians to a set of promises (i.e., policy preferences), and serve as an attractive feature of a politician's character (see, for example, Lott 1987; Dougan and Munger 1989; Hinich and Munger 1996). I have measured such ideological effects by computing the numerical difference between respondent (self) and perceived incumbent placement on an ideological scale running from 1 (very liberal) to 7 (very conservative); this measure is referred to as *ideological congruence*.

A closely related variable is designed to represent the ability of incumbents to engender partisan identification with voters—another alternative or substitute for a faithful-agent reputation. *Partisan congruence* measures whether or not respondents share the same party affiliation as an incumbent senator or representative. There is little argument that party identification—despite its declining influence in recent decades (see, for instance, Wattenberg 1998)—remains a potent influence in congressional elections. Legislators may invoke partisan feelings by encouraging constituents to see them as "at war" with the opposition party, and defending principles and values dear to their voters. Unlike ideological reputations, partisan reputations bind politicians to the pursuit of party-related interests and issues. I anticipate a positive sign between this measure of partisan congruence and incumbent vote support.

The role of the economy in congressional elections remains intensely debated (see, for instance, Kramer 1971; Fiorina 1978; Jacobson 1990a; Erikson 1990) and appears resilient to any easy resolution. Thankfully, the issues raised in this debate are beyond the scope of this inquiry. Nevertheless, I incorporate a measure of perceived economic well-being into the analysis to assure that the effects of economic conditions are not ignored. Economic well-being reflects a message that incumbents frequently spout, and they are not reticent about associating themselves with improvements in economic conditions (see, for example, Tufte 1978). I refer to this variable as *personal finances*; it is a summary indicator of a respondent's present financial state as compared to a year earlier.[2]

A major predictor of congressional election outcomes is the popularity of the incumbent (*incumbent popularity*) among his or her constituents. In fact, the popularity of the incumbent may be the single best predictor of electoral support (Parker 1981; Cain et al. 1987; Parker 1989). Popular incumbents may see little need to cultivate a reputation for trustworthiness: they may view their attractive personality or charisma as substitutes for the vote-earning power of a faithful-agent reputation. A reputation for being a personable, good fellow is the only attribute that some voters like (or perhaps know) about their legislator. The inclusion of this variable in the analysis also assures that the effects of trustworthiness are not merely capturing the positive affect commonly associated with visibility and candidate awareness (Stokes and Miller 1962), or respondent rationalizations for vote decisions. The measure of incumbent popularity is the "feeling thermometer" included in ANES surveys.[3]

As a result of Fenno's personal observations of, and travels with, incumbent Congressmen (Fenno 1978), additional reputational signals can be identified. First, legislators seek to develop reputations for accessibility to constituents. "The more accessible they are, House members believe, the more will their constituents be encouraged to feel that they can communicate with the congressman when and if they wish" (Fenno 1978, 240). Cain and his colleagues (1987, 135–148) measured this element of a legislator's reputation in terms of respondent evaluations as to how helpful a legislator would have been if the respondent had sought help in dealing with a problem. I employ the same variable (*perceived accessibility*), and also introduce two conceptually related measures: the extent to which legislators are seen as "*keeping in touch*" with constituents,[4] and the degree to which constituents have had *personal contact* with their legislator. Personal contact, as noted earlier, creates "extended dealings" (with legislators) that form the basis for the transmission of information relevant to a legislator's reputation. My measure of this personal contact is the sum of the contacts that a respondent reports having had with the incumbent legislator — personally met, attended a meeting where the incumbent spoke, or talked to someone in the congressional office.

Second, one of the major messages legislators communicate to their constituents is to encourage the latter to see them as closely following voter opinion in their policy decisions in Washington. "In justifying their policy decisions," Fenno (1978, 160) writes, "representatives sometimes claim that their policy decisions follow not what they want but what their constituents want." In this way, incumbents legitimatize their votes by contending that they are behaving like "delegates." If such arguments are successful, voters should see little discrepancy between their own policy views and the voting decisions of their legislators. The image or reputation of a legislator as a delegate is measured through an item asking respondents the extent to which they agree or disagree with the way the incumbent has generally voted on legislation in Washington (*perceived voting agreement*).[5]

Third, legislators cultivate perceptions of trust and service to the district, and reputations to match. Measures of *trust* and *constituency service* are drawn from open-ended questions eliciting voter "likes" and "dislikes" of incumbent representatives and senators. Finally, I include measures of other reputations in the analysis that are similarly related to legislator presentations to assure that the effects of trustworthiness on electoral support are not merely capturing the influence of these other reputational signals. These measures relate to the incumbent's *experience, personal characteristics*, and (domestic and foreign) *policy positions*,[6] and provide bases for substitute and constituency-specific reputations; voter likes and dislikes also have been categorized to represent these reputations.

As alluded to earlier in this chapter, there is reason to expect institutional differences in the effects of perceptions of trust on the elections of senators and representatives. Since the six-year Senate term provides ample time for constituents to forget about their senator's misdeeds, senators may feel a less pressing need to make large investments in their reputations for trustworthiness. Candidates challenging incumbent senators might want to make ethical conduct a campaign issue, but they will have to incur large costs to collect and disseminate information about incumbents' cheating—accusations that may be totally disbelieved either because they are made in the midst of election campaigning, or because they are advanced by the political opposition. And, as noted earlier, the enviable ability of senators to obtain prestigious post-elective employment, irrespective of their reputations, reduces their incentives to invest heavily in reputational capital. Taken together, these observations lead to the hypothesis that trustworthiness is more important to the elections of representatives than senators. The shorter "repurchase" period (i.e., two-year term), and the need to appear trustworthy not merely to win reelection—after all, reelection can be obtained in less costly ways (see chapter 3)—but also to attract good jobs once they leave office, make reputational capital a greater concern to members of the House. Consequently, trustworthiness is less likely to be on the voters' minds when deciding who to support in Senate elections: they have probably forgotten the misdeeds of incumbent senators, or perhaps don't care, and the latter have few incentives to make trustworthiness an issue in their campaigns because of their relatively small investments in reputational capital.

THE IMPACT OF TRUSTWORTHINESS ON VOTING IN HOUSE AND SENATE ELECTIONS

Table 6.1 presents the statistical (logit) estimates predicting incumbent support in House and Senate elections. Logit analysis is a maximum likelihood estimation technique appropriate for the analysis of binary dependent variables. The purpose of this analysis is not to assess the effects of individual variables on voter choice, but rather, to evaluate the extent to which constituent perceptions of legislator trustworthiness in-

TABLE 6.1
Predicting Electoral Support for U.S. Representatives and Senators: 1988–1990

Variable	House Logit Estimates[a]	Senate Logit Estimates[a]
Year	−.20	.19
	(−1.24)	(.68)
Personal Finances	.06	.004
	(.61)	(.02)
Ideological Congruence	.33**	.05
	(4.81)	(.04)
Partisan Congruence	1.95**	1.85**
	(10.21)	(6.04)
Incumbent Popularity	.05**	.05**
	(11.21)	(6.32)
Perceived Accessibility	.43*	.20
	(1.97)	(.49)
Trust	.44*	.52
	(1.86)	(1.58)
Personal Contact	.12	1.65**
	(1.48)	(8.20)
Keeping in Touch	.09	.51
	(.70)	(1.26)
Experience	.34	−.47
	(1.21)	(−1.23)
Personal Characteristics	.34	.35
	(1.16)	(.80)
Constituency Service	.27	−.45
	(1.60)	(−1.67)
Perceived Voting Agreement	.46**	.97**
	(2.90)	(3.89)
Domestic Policy Positions	.57*	1.09**
	(2.47)	(2.97)
Foreign Policy Positions	−.12	−.18
	(−.20)	(−.38)
Constant	−2.38**	−5.76**
	(5.72)	(7.60)
Number of Cases	1818	863
Summary statistics:		
Chi-square	947.08	661.43
Degrees of freedom	15	15
	(p < .001)	(p < .001)
Percent improvement over chance	57%	68%

Source: National Election Studies, Senate Elections in Context 1988–1990 Pooled File.
**$p ≤ .01$ one-tailed significance test.
*$p ≤ .05$ one-tailed significance test.
[a]t-values given in parentheses.

fluence such decisions despite the existence of alternative voting cues. Nevertheless, it is impossible to ignore the electoral value of these alternative cues. If legislators are looking for ways to divert the attention of their voters away from questions of propriety, emphasizing partisanship and likeability are two good options (table 6.1). And calling attention to positions on domestic issues, and the accurate representation of district and state opinion, work equally well. Despite these potent voting cues, trust remains an important consideration in voter choice, but only in House elections; it apparently has no significant effects on voting in Senate contests. The types of variables included in the equations are similar to those in other studies of voting in House and Senate elections, and the explanatory power of the equations compares favorably to other models of voting in congressional elections (see, for example, Jacobson 1987, 126; Krasno 1994, 119). Consequently, it is unlikely that the effects of trust in promoting support in House elections are due to important variables being excluded from the explanatory equations. Clearly, trustworthiness is an important electoral asset, but it is not singularly decisive in congressional elections, and it is of little relevance to voting in Senate races.

It might be suggested that the reputational variables based upon likes and dislikes contain little substance, and only reflect affective feelings toward one's legislator or perhaps rationalizations; hence, any relationship between measurements based upon likes and dislikes might be merely capturing the extent to which popular candidates are reelected! However, there is evidence suggesting that even when the effects of such rationalizations are taken into account, the reputation of an incumbent, for, say, constituent "helpfulness," affects his or her electoral success (Romero 1996). Moreover, the inclusion of incumbent popularity into the equations predicting voting in House and Senate elections demonstrates that more than affect is associated with perceptions of trustworthiness. Although trust is significant (House data), its effect is dwarfed by other variables in both the House and the Senate data. And, as expected, trustworthiness is less important to the electoral vote of senators. But these data only refer to the vote in discrete elections, and reputational capital is a long-term asset. Indeed, I have assumed that reputational capital provides a long-term earnings stream. Perhaps such capital is more significant to the over-time electoral survival of faithful agents?

The Careers Prospects for Faithful Agents

We can gain another perspective on the electoral value of a faithful-agent reputation by considering the relationship between reputational capital and the departures of House incumbents. I have recoded the measurement of the reputational capital of House incumbents (see chapter 4) into five distinct categories to facilitate tabular analysis: (1) distrust (negative ratings); (2) less than 5 percent of district voters see their representative as a faithful agent; (3) between 6 and 10 percent of district voters see their representative as a faithful agent; (4) between 11 and 20 percent of district voters see their representative as a faithful agent; (5) more than 20 percent of district voters see their representative as a faithful agent. These categories can be viewed as reflecting the incumbent's goodwill among constituents—the greater the breadth, the greater the strength of the incumbent's reputation within his or her constituency. Dougan and Munger (1989, 128) contend that "an incumbent actively seeking a reputation for honesty is unlikely to survive politically." If they are correct, an important incentive for reputational control may be doomed.

Table 6.2 describes the reasons given for exiting the House of Representatives. Surprisingly, there are no major differences at the extreme levels of faithfulness: neither the least nor the most trusted representatives exit office more frequently through electoral defeat. Nonetheless, legislators with "average" or "above average" levels of reputational capital exit office far less frequently due to electoral defeat than those with "below average" levels of reputational capital. One-third of the legislators with "below average" levels of trustworthiness exited the House because they lost an election, while only 12.8 percent of the legislators with "above average" levels of faithfulness left for the same reason. In short, reputational capital seems to enhance long-term electoral survival.

Why do the *most* faithful leave office through electoral defeat at the same rate as the *least* faithful? Perhaps the most faithful are occasionally too *principled* for their principals—namely, the voters. That is, faithful agents are not merely trustworthy; they are also very likely to be principled. The two attributes—honesty and principles—are frequently linked in the public's perceptions of faithful representatives; however, the moral imperatives or principles followed by a legislator may occasionally clash with the parochial interests of constituents. Such deviance is probably tolerated most of the time by voters who consider it part of the cost required in having a faithful agent. Nonetheless, issues may arise where a legislator's principles or desires to "do the right thing" anger a significant segment of the constituency, resulting in the electoral defeat of an exceptionally trustworthy representative. For example, suppose a very faithful agent believed that it was in the best interests of *all* citizens—those both within and outside of the district—to reduce federal programs, several of which specifically benefited pow-

TABLE 6.2
Why Do Faithful Agents Exit Office?

Reason for Exiting House of Representatives	Net Level of Reputational Capital				
	Disliked (negative rating)	Below Average (≤5%)	Average (6%–10%)	Above Average (11%–19%)	High (≥20%)
Retirement	46.2%	26.7%	52.6%	30.8%	41.2%
Lost election	30.8	33.3	21.1	12.8	35.3
Successful run for another office	7.7	6.7	5.3	10.3	—
Unsuccessful run for another office	15.4	16.7	13.2	23.1	11.8
Death	—	6.7	5.3	15.4	11.8
Appointment to another office	—	10.0	2.6	7.7	—
Number of cases	13	30	38	39	17

erful district interests. The expected intensity of group feelings over this issue may be sufficient to overcome or offset the legislator's reservoir of reputational goodwill. In sum, the lesson here is that faithful agents may, on occasion, be too principled for the voters' appetite. Perhaps more importantly, this result suggests that electoral safety may be a less significant reward for trustworthy politicians than imagined. The "premium" paid faithful agents once they *leave Congress* (post-elective employment) may, in contrast, loom as a far more consequential incentive for ethical conduct.

The issue of reelection aside, does a faithful-agent reputation provide a "safety net" for legislators who find themselves "out of a job"? In the remainder of this chapter, I examine whether a reputation as a faithful agent helps the electorally unsuccessful obtain attractive post-elective employment. I beg the reader's indulgence at this stage of the analysis since it is extremely difficult to obtain reliable and complete information on the post-elective employment of legislators; thus the categorization of attractive post-elective employment opportunities is at best a crude measure. I have been quite generous, once again, in defining vocations that constitute prestigious or attractive post-elective employment; otherwise, the number of House members receiving prestigious employment would be pathetically low. It is doubtful that my liberal definition strengthens the relationship between reputational capital and prestigious post-elective employment. It is more likely that the imprecision of measurement attenuates the relationship. I have placed exclusive reliance upon *The Biographical Directory of the American Congress,*

1774–1996 (Congressional Quarterly 1997) for information on the post-elective employment of representatives and senators. Despite the accuracy of the information contained in this document, the details of post-elective employment remain sketchy. (A list of post-elective employment positions considered to be prestigious can be found in appendix 5.)

As hypothesized, faithful agents have a better chance of obtaining prestigious post-elective employment than the less faithful (table 6.3). Highly trusted House incumbents, repudiated at the polls, are more than twice as likely to obtain prestigious post-elective employment than the least faithful members. Unfortunately, even among the most faithful (category 5) the probability of obtaining attractive post-elective employment is modest at best (37.5%). This is rather surprising in light of the high levels of trustworthiness associated with legislators in this group. In short, if faithful agents are unsuccessful in gaining reelection, or seeking higher office, they have a better chance than the less faithful of obtaining prestigious post-elective employment, but their chances still remain less than 50–50.

While reputational trust may enhance post-elective employment, its effects could be counterbalanced by other legislator attributes of equally marketable value. To explore this possibility, I examine the partial eta statistics associated with three basic legislator attributes — party, seniority (year elected to the House), and years of service in prior public office — along with the measure of reputational capital. The research question is whether faithful agents have an advantage in obtaining prestigious post-elective employment, irrespective of basic legislator characteristics. Table 6.4 describes the findings.

The *partial eta-squared statistic* provides a measure of the relative importance of variables. This statistic indicates that reputational capital is far-and-away the most important factor explaining post-elective employment. Indeed, it is almost twice the size of the next most important variable (i.e., years in prior public office). Admittedly, the effects of reputational capital in explaining post-elective employment remain small, but they are, nonetheless, considerably more important than other basic legislator characteristics that should have some asset value for attractive post-elective employment. This observation should cause us to pause before we minimize the effects of reputational capital on post-elective employment, since reputational capital is greater than political party affiliation, seniority, and years of prior public officeholding, in enhancing the prospects for attractive employment. In sum, there is evidence that "premiums" are paid to faithful agents, at least in the House of Representatives: trust affects the electoral votes and long-term survival of incumbent representatives, and when the latter lose office, they are

TABLE 6.3
Does a Reputation Make a Difference in Post-Elective Employment for Those Who Lost Reelection?

	Net Level of Reputational Capital				
Status of Post-Election Position	Disliked (Negative rating)	Below Average (≤5%)ᵃ	Average (6%–10%)	Above Average (11%–19%)	High (≥20%)
Exiting legislator attained prestigious post-elective position	16.7%	13.3%	15.4%	28.6%	37.5%
Exiting legislator did not attain prestigious post-elective position	83.3	86.7	84.6	71.4	62.5
Number of cases	6	15	13	14	8

ᵃNumbers in parentheses refer to the percentage of each legislator's pooled sample who recognize him or her as having a reputation as a good (or poor) agent. These percentages have been collapsed into the perspective categories for the purpose of tabular presentation.

Statistics:
  Kendall's Tau-b = .17
  Kendall's Tau-c = .18
  Gamma = .33

more successful than the less faithful in obtaining attractive post-elective employment.

WHY CORRUPT POLITICIANS DON'T FEAR ELECTORAL REPRISAL

In light of what we have said so far, untrustworthy legislators, especially those involved in scandals, stand to lose reputational capital and therefore electoral support with some degree of frequency. While correct, we should not leap to the conclusion that elections are therefore potent instruments for ridding the institution of some of its most dishonest members. Although we can take solace in the fact that reputational capital is an important election and post-election (employment) asset, it is clear from the data in table 6.1 that it is not the sole, or even a major, determinant of voter choice in congressional elections; hence, voter trust is not a sufficient condition for electoral success. This is not unexpected. What is rather surprising is that trustworthiness isn't even essential for

Table 6.4
The Importance of Reputational Capital in Obtaining Prestigious Post-Elective
Employment upon Electoral Defeat

Variables	Partial Eta Squared
Years of prior public officeholding	.025
Party	.001
Year elected	.009
Net reputational capital[a]	.045
Number of cases	56

[a]Reputational capital is categorized in the following manner:
  −3.50–2.80 = 1
  2.90–8.40 = 2
  8.50–15.50 = 3
  15.70–35.00 = 4

keeping legislators in office. That is, scandalized legislators are unusually adept at staying in office. In the following pages I suggest why.

Before discussing why scandalized politicians are reelected, it is important to gauge the latter's level of electoral success to see how reluctant voters really are about tossing *their* rascals out. The evidence is rather convincing. For example, John Peters and Susan Welch (1980), analyzing instances of corruption between 1968 and 1978 as they related to the congressional vote, found that while some candidates accused of corruption simply retired or chose not to seek reelection, more than two-thirds of those running in the general election were successful (Peters and Welch 1980, 703, table 1). Susan Welch and John Hibbing (1997) extended the time frame and found a similar electoral success rate for incumbents charged with corruption between 1982 and 1990. Of course the success rate of corrupt politicians remains significantly lower than that of honest legislators:

> 65% of corruption-charged incumbents appear in the next Congress, while 72% of those attempting to secure reelection (primary and general combined) are successful. These figures are very similar for the 1968–1978 period where 61% of corruption-charged incumbents appeared in the next Congress while 70% of those attempting to secure reelection were successful. And these rates are substantially lower than we find for House members in the 1980s not charged with scandal. Fully 85% of "clean members" returned to the next Congress. If we limit the analysis to only those who tried to return to the next Congress, the figure is 92%. (Welch and Hibbing 1997, 233–234)

Although incumbents charged with corruption are about nine times more likely to lose reelection than a legislator not similarly tainted (Peters and Welch 1980, 233),[7] corrupt politicians are not easily turned out of office since better than two of every three return for another term.

Anticipatory Retirement

One obvious explanation for why corrupt politicians seem to return in such alarming numbers is that those who are the most corrupt retire before they have to face the electorate. This could exaggerate the electoral survival of corrupt legislators, since only those able to withstand charges of corruption, or effectively combat them, attempt to seek reelection. Thus, *retirements* on the part of ethically challenged legislators need to be added to the costs of corruption. However, there is evidence that even charges of corruption may not encourage legislators to retire. For instance, revelations that legislators kited checks at the House bank caused a few incumbents to retire but not very many (Groseclose and Krehbiel 1994, 92).[8] Questions of ethical propriety may force a few legislators into premature retirement, but many more take their chances at the polls, which isn't a risky bet.

Nature of the Charges

Another factor that needs to be considered in explaining the minimal effects associated with charges of corruption is the nature of the charges themselves. For example, while 38.2 percent of the respondents, who reported voting in contests between a challenger and an incumbent in the 1992 congressional elections, agreed with the statement "Representatives who wrote bad checks acted so dishonestly they should be voted out of office," a majority of respondents either did not have an opinion (9.7%), believed that writing a few bad checks was acceptable (31.3%),[9] or were convinced that the action was not a serious enough mistake to warrant disqualification (20.8%)[10] (Miller et al. 1993).

This lack of enthusiasm for punishing transgressions can be seen in the effects of check kiting on electoral support: Approximately 60 percent of the voters in 1992 supported incumbent candidates who had kited 100 or more checks (table 6.5). It might be argued that the bank scandal and the associated check kiting were rather minor events that escaped public notice, and therefore were unlikely to register anything but a mild tremor at election time. However, more than nine of ten respondents (93.8%) acknowledged having "read or heard about the U.S. representatives writing checks when they didn't have enough money to cover them in their House bank accounts" (Miller et al.

TABLE 6.5
Checks Kited and Electoral Support for Incumbent

Number of Overdrafts	Percentage Voting for Incumbent
None	74.2
1–49	73.1
50–99	77.8
100–199	64.4
200 or more	58.5
Number of cases	1007

Source: American National Elections Study (Miller et al. 1993).

Note: Percentages based on responses of the 1,007 respondents who reported voting in contests between an incumbent and a challenger in 1992 congressional elections.

1993). It surely was not a lack of information that mitigated electoral reprisals aimed at check-kiters. Indeed, even challengers, who faced incumbents that were perceived by the voters to have written "a lot" of overdrafts, were only able to obtain a bare majority vote (table 6.6).

This lack of electoral retribution is not simply a result of the fact that opportunism is more unethical than illegal. For instance, charges of conflict of interest do not seem to engender much electoral retribution either; only morals charges and bribery seem to have any measurable impact on voter support (Peters and Welch 1980, 705, table 3).[11] In short, the lack of electoral retribution aimed at corrupt legislators may be a consequence of the inability of the *charges* to excite much anger among voters.

Barriers to Entry

Competition in elections might seem an appropriate institutional mechanism for constraining opportunism, but barriers to entry diminish electoral competition by enhancing the advantages of incumbency and deterring quality candidates from challenging incumbents (Parker 1992). The ability of incumbents to provide services to constituents is an example of a barrier to the entry of effective competition since only incumbents can provide the service and gain recognition for doing so (Parker 1981; Fiorina and Noll 1979). Constituents are virtually silent about the constituency attentiveness of those who challenge incumbents but quite vocal about the constituency service supplied by incumbents (Parker 1986). This is one characteristic that differentiates between candidates to the advantage of incumbents, and because most service receives high marks from constituents, the provision of constituency services enhances the standing of members of Congress among their voters.

Table 6.6
Perceptions of Opportunism and Electoral Support for Incumbents

Perceptions of Incumbent's Opportunism[a]	Percentage Voting for Incumbent
Incumbent wrote no overdrafts	80.7
Incumbent wrote a few overdrafts	71.3
Incumbent wrote a lot of overdrafts	49.1
Unaware if incumbent wrote overdrafts	69.5
Number of cases	1007

Source: American National Election Study (Miller et al. 1993).
Note: Percentages based on responses of the 1,007 respondents who reported voting in elections between an incumbent and a challenger in 1992 congressional elections.
[a]Responses are based on the following series of questions:
  1. "Did [name of representative] write any bad checks?"
  2. [If yes] "Did [name of representative] write a lot of bad checks or just a few?"
Respondents who believed their representative to have written some bad checks, but were uncertain as to whether they numbered "a few" or "a lot," were placed in the former category (i.e., few checks).

Thus, the monopoly over bureaucratic fix-it services exercised by incumbents raises a barrier to the entry of electoral challenges.

In addition, most of the costs associated with the provision and advertising of these services are subsidized by the government (Parker 1992, 17, table 1); this raises the barriers to entry even higher by increasing the costs of campaigning for those challenging incumbents. Incumbents can campaign on a daily basis and be paid for doing so, the legislative schedule is adjusted so that time spent in the district does not detract from legislators' interests, and the costs associated with district service can be imposed on others (e.g., staff). Not only have incumbents cornered the market on ombudsmen services for constituents, but the advertising and provision of these services are subsidized by the government. Government subsidies have enabled incumbents to increase their advertising, which has resulted in an increased demand for their services and a reduction in the elasticity of that demand. As a result, the demand for legislator's services expands, and the decline in elasticity intensifies constituent preferences for incumbents, thereby assuring a reliable core of supporters and safe reelection margins (Parker 1992).

Lack of Information

Another reason unethical legislators survive electoral challenges is because voters normally lack information about the behavior of their legislators and rarely have incentives to overcome their rational ignorance. The costs of information assure a minimal flow to voters, and create obstacles to identifying legislative misdeeds. Even when charges are leveled against an incumbent, will voters believe them? Since candidates know that most citizens are repulsed by political corruption, each has an incentive to label the other as corrupt and to defend themselves from such charges. Thus, charges of corruption leveled by opposing candidates — the most likely sources of such information — lack credibility because they are self-serving and likely to be disputed. In short, the lack of information, or the distortions built into information by rational, enterprising candidates, lead voters to be ignorant of the illegal or unethical activities of incumbent politicians, or at least uncertain about the validity of accusations of wrongdoing.

Voter Self-Interest

Rather than blaming the reelection of unethical or corrupt politicians on voter ignorance, the voters may be *consciously* electing dishonest politicians. The venality of some constituents leads them to vote for candidates who will exchange material benefits for electoral support. Simply put, some voters support politicians who are eager to traffic in material benefits (e.g., patronage jobs, licenses) in return for votes. Bringing unnecessary federal projects to the district, or doing political favors, may be ethically questionable in some respects, but for voters gaining from such federal largess, or the particularized benefits resulting from some favor, there is nothing but glowing words and approbation for those who deliver the "bacon." Since most incumbents perform admirably in these tasks, they are in a good position to persuade constituents to keep them in office regardless of their transgressions.[12] Therefore, voters may tolerate, and even enthusiastically support, politicians who are adept at meeting their material demands, regardless of the latters' lack of propriety.

Importance in Vote Decision

Charges of corruption may not be given much weight because such charges are only one of many factors influencing congressional elections. For example, Michael Dimock and Gary Jacobson (1995, 1149) include a measure of check-kiting behavior (i.e., number of overdrafts) within a nine-variable equation to explain voting in House elections in 1992. Amid such a complex set of factors influencing voter decisions, charges of corruption might easily be lost or relegated to a lower level of importance. Moreover,

if candidate corruption is treated like any other component in the voter's choice between two candidates, it follows that there are conditions under which a rational voter would knowingly support corrupt candidates. He would do so if he perceived both candidates as corrupt, or if he decides that a corrupt candidate who is closer to his own preferences on other issues is preferable to a "clean" candidate who is not. In either case, he would vote for the corrupt candidate because the candidate shares or is closer to his own political preferences. (Rundquist, Strom, and Peters 1977, 956)

And if the alleged corrupt act was minor, it may be given short shrift in the voting decision. For instance, the bank scandal left little more than a chemical trace on voter decisions in the 1992 House elections (Jacobson and Dimock 1994; Alford et al. 1994).

Only if voters feel strongly about honesty and trustworthiness can we expect charges of corruption to make a difference. If voters place a greater emphasis on the political party affiliation of the candidates, or their stands on salient issues, charges of corruption may be treated like other forms of "dirt" — it doesn't damage the product, only its luster. Moreover, if voters are indifferent to corruption because of a distrust of politicians and/or adverse selection in the candidate pool, such charges are unlikely to leave much of a mark on the electoral fate of politicians who are exposed as unethical or opportunistic.

Rationalizations

There is another closely related reason for voters to discount charges of corruption in their voting decisions that stems from the fact that constituents tend to "love" their representatives (Parker and Davidson 1979), and to rationalize their foibles and excesses. Intense personal commitments by those in a legislator's electoral following serve to screen out charges leveled against a beloved legislator. Thus, dissonance-reducing rationales may develop among those loyal to a legislator that prevent ethical transgressions from negating voter loyalties. This seems to be the case in the check-kiting scandal: voter opinions on check kiting served more to rationalize than to mold electoral decisions.

Michael Dimock and Gary Jacobson (1995) observed that voters who knew and liked their representatives were less inclined to take a hard-line position on writing overdrafts at the House bank than were voters less endeared to their representatives. The incumbent's partisans, and those who knew and appreciated the incumbent's performance at home and in Washington, took a more lenient view of check-kiting behavior and were predisposed to assume innocence. In this way, voters reduced the dissonance between their positive feelings toward their representative and the latter's check-kiting behavior:

Fortunately for members with a record of bad checks, voters who knew about it were least inclined to be outraged by it, while the voters who were most disposed to punish the offense were also the least disposed to believe that their representatives had written bad checks, even when they had. The main reason for this pattern is that voters who faced the option of condemning an incumbent they otherwise appreciated for writing bad checks or dismissing the offense as inconsequential often chose the latter course. The damage was also moderated by partisanship; voters identifying with the incumbent's party showed a strong tendency to err in his or her favor in assessing involvement in the scandal. (Dimock and Jacobson 1995, 1157)

A similar point is made by John Alford and his colleagues (Alford et al. 1994), who suggest that the House bank scandal had little effect on the 1992 elections because voters discounted the culpability of their own members for a scandal that they believed to be endemic to the institution. "Voters viewed the scandal as an institutional problem embedded in Congress, rather than focused on their particular member" (Alford et al. 1994, 799). Thus the blame was diffused. Voters may have been totally disgusted with "the institution," but they could not bring themselves to either punish or blame their own legislator for behaving like everyone else. Given the moral hazards surrounding the exploitation of many congressional prerogatives (e.g., foreign travel, honoraria), voters with inclinations to rationalize away charges of ethical transgressions will have ample opportunities to do so. We should not be too surprised, then, that so few electoral casualties can be linked to acts of opportunism.[13]

To summarize, charges of corruption can unseat dishonest politicians but the effects may be muted by a variety of conditions that confront voters—attachments to offending candidates, lack of information, the nature of the violation, the existence of barriers to competition and the like. Although elections can operate to rid institutions of those who would exploit their public positions for personal gain, they are imperfect instruments of ex post enforcement that put the onus on those—voters—who show some reluctance to exercise this responsibility.

CONCLUSION

Clearly, a reputation as a faithful agent is an electoral asset, but you don't need to be highly trusted to be electorally successful. High levels of trust or distrust make little difference in the probability of exiting office due to electoral defeat, although moderate levels of reputational capital induce far greater levels of electoral security. These findings seem to echo those derived from the analysis of the election data: reputational capital is an asset but there are other factors that operate on elections, and the latter may do so in such a fashion that mitigates some of the electoral benefit derived from a faithful-agent reputation.

Kalt and Zupan (1984) suggest that opportunism (i.e., shirking in voting) declines as the "policemen" — elections — approach, and there is evidence that elections serve as ex post mechanisms for enforcing conduct and punishing transgressions. Those involved in scandals and acts of corruption lose election at higher rates than honest politicians. Still, the analysis suggests that unethical behavior, whether or not it even reaches the ears of voters, is not a dominant consideration in vote choice. Thus elections, like warranties, are imperfect ex post instruments of quality control and must be supplemented with other mechanisms and institutions to be truly effective.

Building reputational capital still seems rational. Even if its effects on elections are somewhat muted, such capital will cushion any departure from Congress, at least for House incumbents. Unfortunately, these relationships do not hold for senators. The electoral survival of faithful agents suggests that reputational capital is a long-run asset. This is consistent with the proposition that to be an effective deterrent to unethical behavior, reputational capital must supply a long-term earnings stream for trustworthy legislators. If legislators keep their reputations clean they can anticipate a handsome premium: long legislative careers and prestigious jobs should they lose office.

CHAPTER 7

Weaknesses in Reputational Controls

IN THIS CHAPTER I examine weaknesses in the reputational control of opportunistic behavior. I have suggested that refraining from opportunistic behavior builds reputational capital, but this is not the only way of increasing such capital; reputational capital is also enhanced through the extended dealings of legislators. Among consumers, as well as constituents, reputations spread through the pooling of information based upon personal experiences. With this effect in mind, perhaps, legislators expend considerable effort maintaining personal contact with constituents in order to cultivate perceptions of trustworthiness (Fenno 1978). Taken together, these observations lead to the hypothesis that constituent contacts with representatives and senators "slant" the acquired information, thereby enhancing perceptions of trustworthiness, and as these perceptions are shared with others, building reputational capital. This ensures that the circulation of information acquired through personal contacts with constituents will be biased in favor of legislators, thereby diminishing the force of the extended dealings of legislators in constraining unethical conduct. In addition to the informational bias resulting from personal contact with legislators, reputational controls encounter difficulties with each successive step in the ladder of governmental power.

Senators and presidents face different costs and benefits than House incumbents. Senators, for instance, have an easier time finding prestigious jobs once they leave office than representatives (appendix 6), and their electoral fortunes are less influenced by perceptions of trustworthiness (chapter 6). These differences should make senators, and presidents for that matter, less committed to making large investments in reputational capital. This leads to the specific proposition that the more powerful the political office, the lower the demand for reputational capital — a negative relationship between institutional power and reputational capital. That is, the higher the political office, the greater the visibility, contacts, and prominence, and thus the less reputational capital necessary to obtain attractive post-elective employment; ergo, the higher the political office, the fewer the incentives to invest in one's reputation.

The irony here is that as you progress up the ladder of political power, and reputational capital declines, the need to control malfeasance actually increases because of the power of the office, and therefore the private gain that can be expropriated. Reputational capital is a necessary supplement to existing mechanisms for controlling politicians, but its effectiveness may decline with each successive step up the ladder of political power in the U.S. government. There is another threat to the effectiveness of reputational capital in controlling the opportunistic appetites of legislators: incumbent advertising may blind voters to weaknesses in character.

ARE VOTERS FOOLED BY LEGISLATOR ADVERTISING?

Reputational capital would have no measureable effect in constraining unethical conduct if legislators could convince constituents of their trustworthiness by merely engaging in some form of self-promotion, or as Mayhew (1974) has dubbed it, "advertising." In economics, "advertising may signal a certain level of quality. A well-known article, one that has been advertised and on the market for a long time, is more likely to yield satisfactory service than one about which little is known or one with which consumers must experiment. Therefore consumers may justifiably regard the risk of using the advertised product to be less than the risk of using the non-advertised product" (Telser 1964, 539). As mentioned in chapter 2, the less informed might come to trust a legislator because of name familiarity and the size of his or her electoral following. Since "advertising" is a major preoccupation of legislators (Mayhew 1974), we might expect the same relationship to transpire: legislator advertising serves to convince constituents of their trustworthiness and dutiful service.

In the economic sphere, firms producing high-quality brands expend greater effort to persuade consumers to try their wares, since *ceteris paribus*, the present value of a trial purchase is larger because high-quality goods obtain more repeat purchases than low-quality goods. Some economists contend that quality information is provided by the *level of advertising*, not merely the claims it makes (Nelson 1974). Yet, if buyers are known to be responsive to advertising expenditures, low-quality products will advertise enough to more than overcome their rivals' greater ability to hold customers. Therefore, advertising levels can mislead buyers (Schmalensee 1978).

Voters seem smarter with respect to the advertising of their legislators: There is no evidence that levels of reputational capital are built through mere exposure.[1] It is plausible that reputational capital might increase in response to the frequency with which legislators visit their

TABLE 7.1
Are Reputations for Trustworthiness Built through Exposure?

Legislator's Activity	Correlation with Reputational Capital	Level of Significance[a]
Number of years in political office prior to congressional service	−.10 (211)[b]	.081
Total time spent in the district: 1981–1994	−.05 (211)	.232
Seniority	.07 (211)	.172

[a]One-tailed significance level test.
[b]Numbers in parentheses refer to number of cases upon which statistics are calculated.

constituencies, or the length of time in office. The more voters see and hear from their politicians, for example, the greater the likelihood that they will see the latter as highly reputable. Neither of these specific relationships are observed, however (table 7.1). For instance, the total number of days spent in the district (or the number of days per year) is unrelated to reputational capital (table 7.1). Nor is the supply of reputational capital enhanced by a political career and the extensive advertising that occurs along with it. Cain and his colleagues (1987, 146–147) reached a similar conclusion about reputations for constituency service: "Overall there is little support for the notion that constituency reputation simply increases with every year in office."

Legislator advertising may be less important in promoting reputational goodwill because voters rely more upon others to provide them with information relevant to evaluating the faithfulness of their agents. In the economic sphere, consumers place considerable reliance upon the advice of relatives and friends in their purchases because they believe that these recommendations constitute better information than advertising. "Certainly these recommendations must sometimes provide better information or they would never be used. The consumer is surrounded by a sea of advertising whose information is obtained by the consumer at virtually no cost to himself. The consumer, then, always has the alternative of using advertising as his guide. Instead he sometimes uses the guidance of relatives and friends. Hence, that information must sometimes be better information. The more consumers use relatives and friends, the less they respond to advertising" (Nelson 1974, 747). If voters react in a similar way to the advertising of their politicians, then we can expect that the activities undertaken by politicians to engender visibility will have little impact on their stock of reputational capital. In short, weaknesses in reputational controls are unlikely to stem from the fact that legislator advertising convinces voters of the trustworthiness of their representative. "Advertising" is not the culprit.

EXTENDED DEALINGS AND REPUTATIONAL CAPITAL

As noted in chapter 2, voters form impressions of the character of public officials on the basis of their own personal contact, or that of others, with these politicians. And voters share their experiences, creating networks of individuals who have had dealings with specific public officials, and willingly spread the "word" to others. I now examine the effects of extended dealings with representatives and senators on reputational trust. The measure of extended dealings is fashioned after the items used to record citizen contact with their representatives and senators in the National Election Studies (Center for Political Studies, University of Michigan), with the addition of another item. I have added an item that records the respondent's awareness of the efforts of others to contact his or her legislator, in order to capture the secondary information derived from the contacts of others — an essential component in the pooling of information. These contact measures form a single dimension: met personally, talked to staff members, know someone who has had contact, attended a speech or rally.[2] That is, all of the variables included in this index are highly intercorrelated, forming a scale which I have characterized as the *extended-dealings index*. As noted in chapter 4, I expect that the more personal and indirect contacts made with a political leader, the higher the level of his or her perceived trust. Low scores on the extended-dealings index reflect less contact.

Reputational trust is measured by responses to four survey items that ask about the honesty and trustworthiness of the respondent's representative and senator — they are honest, keep campaign promises, can be trusted, and do the correct or right thing. These items are described in greater detail in chapter 4. Respondents receive a score of 1 for each trusting response they offer, with the scale (*perceptions of trust*) ranging from 0 (distrusting) to 4 (totally trusting). Measures of reputational trust are created for Florida U.S. Representatives, and Senators Connie Mack (R) and Bob Graham (D).

It is difficult to determine whether the contacts between legislators and their constituents produce information that permits unbiased assessments of trustworthiness because we normally lack a priori information about the reputability of legislators among their voters. Thus, we have no way of knowing whether contacts between voters and their legislators increase the perceived trustworthiness of the latter because

these legislators are actually highly reputable, or merely adept at manip-
ulating these contacts to create goodwill. If we knew beforehand, however, that one legislator had a better reputation for trustworthiness than
another, then we could compare the impact of personal contact on perceptions of trustworthiness to see if such contact benefited the most or
least reputable of the two legislators.

Florida Senators Bob Graham (D) and Connie Mack (R) provide a
case in point since there is a large difference in their reputations for
trustworthiness. In terms of reputational capital (tables 4.1 and 4.2),
Bob Graham ranks first (28.7%), and Connie Mack is among the lowest 20 senators in capital (3%), nestled next to the now infamous Senator Bob Packwood (Oregon). In the data from Florida, a similar pattern
emerges: The mean levels of perceived trustworthiness (on the scale) are
1.70 for Bob Graham and 1.33 for Connie Mack, with larger means
representing higher levels of trust. Indeed, Floridians were more trusting
of President Clinton in 1997 (mean level of perceived trust = 1.53)
than Connie Mack.[3] If Mack is so untrustworthy, dealing with him
should reveal this fact, confirming voters' worst fears and resulting in a
negative relationship between contact and perceived trustworthiness.
Just the opposite should be true for Graham: constituents should view
Graham as more trustworthy as their contacts with him (or his staff)
accumulate. These predictions assume that personal experiences with
legislators reveal information relevant for evaluating their trustworthiness. If, on the other hand, contacts are manipulated so that only perceptions of trustworthiness are nourished, there should be little difference between the impact of contact on the perceived trustworthiness of
Graham and Mack.

Several other explanatory variables, aside from extended dealings, are
also included in the analysis of reputational trustworthiness to avoid
questions of improperly specified models. *System trust*, for one, is measured by asking respondents how often they trust the governments in
Washington, D.C. and Florida to do what is right.[4] These two variables
are combined to tap trusting feelings toward the national and state
(Florida) governments. The expectation is that people who are disgrun-
tled with the national (or state) government might also harbor distrust
toward other levels of government and elected officials. The wording of
these questions is analogous to the wording used in the National Election Surveys: "How much of the time do you think you can trust the
government in Washington, D.C. (Florida) to do what is right—just
about always, most of the time, or only some of the time?" Low values
on the system trust index indicate high levels of distrust.

A second explanatory variable is related to the *perceived impact of
taxes*. It doesn't take an oracle to predict that perceived tax burden is a

prominent consideration in evaluations of incumbent performance. Especially destructive of trust are perceptions that existing taxes are "too high" (see, for example, Sears and Citrin 1985). I measure citizen perceptions of state tax burden based on a series of survey items that ask respondents to evaluate the state taxes they pay — are they too high, too low, or about right?[5] It can be easily argued that opinions on state taxes are apt to color the popularity of state leaders. Indeed, it is a rare event for a governor to raise taxes without sacrificing his or her standing among voters. But do fluctuations in the perceived burden of state taxes affect perceptions of national leaders? It is unlikely that voters would blame national leaders for the effects of state taxes; certainly it is not a very rational response for voters. Therefore, I do not expect evaluations of state tax burden to affect trust of national politicians. Nonetheless, citizen trust in politicians in general might be dampened by the perceived oppressiveness of governmental taxes, with the fallout affecting national as well as state leaders; hence, this hypothesis is too viable to be ignored in developing equations to explain reputational trust. High scores on the evaluation of state tax burden scale represent positive evaluations of the burden created through state taxes.

Economic perceptions have also been found to influence attitudes toward political elites, like presidents. To capture any effect that such views may have on elite evaluations I have included two variables measuring perceptions of the state of the country's economy. It is expected that people who feel that their personal finances are better than in the previous year will rate a leader's performance more favorably than people who feel their finances have deteriorated. Similarly, expectations of better personal finances in the future and a positive view of the country's economy should lead to higher evaluations. The measure of *economic outlook* is the total number of positive evaluations about the economy and economic performance offered by respondents.[6] Low values on this variable represent less optimistic perceptions of personal finances and the economy.

No analysis of political attitudes or behavior would be complete without the inclusion of a variable measuring *partisan affiliation*: Republican, Independent, or Democrat. The influence of party identification normally sets the standard by which individual variables are judged as important. The hypothesis is simply that voters harbor suspicions about the values, beliefs, and interests of politicians from the opposition party. For the analysis of Florida's representatives, party identification measures the congruence between the respondent's party identification and that of his or her representative. With respect to the senators, I have measured the party identification of Florida voters in the standard fashion: strong Republican (1), not so strong Republican (2), closer to Republicans (3), Independent (4), closer to Democrats (5), not so strong Democrat (6), strong Democrat (7). I have also measured partisanship in terms of political issues, but the measures differ in the two surveys. One survey includes questions about the number of issues where the respondent favors the traditional Democratic party position,[7] while the other includes items about the proximity of candidates' and partys' policy positions to those of the respondent.[8] It is unfortunate that identical measures could not be constructed but it is doubtful that the construction of these measures of *issue partisanship* will disturb the effects of the extended dealings of legislators on perceptions of trustworthiness, or confound across institution comparisons. These measures of issue partisanship are only included to account for the fact that party identification may mean less to respondents, especially in the South. Taken together, these measures of partisanship should provide a good representation of the partisan forces operating on the perceptions and attitudes of voters. The remaining variables included in the equations represent standard demographic factors — *income, race, and age*.

Table 7.2 presents the results of regressing (OLS) the measure of perceived trustworthiness on variables representing partisan attitudes, economic perceptions, demographic and personal factors, trust in government in general, and the extent to which individuals have had dealings with their representatives and senators. If we only concentrate attention on the most highly significant variables (significance level $\leq .001$), *system trust* and *extended dealings* are far and away the most important factors promoting reputational trust, and the latter variable is clearly the most critical factor affecting the perceived trustworthiness of Senators Graham (Beta = .246) and Mack (Beta = .265). Past studies have affirmed the important relationship between system trust and trust in members of Congress (Born 1990; Parker and Parker 1993), but despite such very strong effects, extended dealings with legislators remain potent influences on reputational trust.

There are two additional features of this table that warrant mention. First, representatives appear to have no comparative advantage over senators in the effects of personal contact. Although representatives spend more of their personal time than senators attending to constituents and their problems, such contact appears to have less effect on their perceived trustworthiness. Contact with Florida's senators increases perceptions of trustworthiness by more than twice the amount that such contact boosts the perceived trustworthiness of Florida's representatives: The understandardized regression coefficients associated with the extended-dealings index are .158 for representatives, .464 for Senator Mack, and .396 for Senator Graham (table 7.2). Second, although Mack has no valid claim to a reputation for trustworthiness,

TABLE 7.2
Contact with Legislators and Perceptions of Trust

Explanatory Variables	U.S. Representatives			Senator Connie Mack			Senator Bob Graham		
	b	Beta	t	b	Beta	t	b	Beta	t
Party identification	.008	.006	.123	-.119***	-.176	-3.662	-.071*	-.103	-2.137
Preference for Democratic issue positions	.057	.050	1.081	.029	.046	.968	.088**	.135	2.862
Perceived state tax burden	.090	.064	1.355	.052	.037	1.061	.045	.031	.896
Economic outlook	.037	.031	.614	.119**	.087	2.449	.118*	.084	2.391
Household income	.014	.026	.518	.039**	.091	2.629	.018	.043	1.245
Race	-.066	-.016	-.336	-.129	-.027	-.788	-.265	-.055	-1.591
Age	.003	.049	.959	.007**	.094	2.657	.010**	.123	3.448
Extended-dealings index	.158***	.182	3.836	.464***	.265	8.114	.396***	.246	7.459
System trust	.539***	.353	7.606	.322***	.167	5.143	.416***	.212	6.529
R Square		.174			.166			.164	
Number of cases		400			833			833	

*.05 level of significance (two-tailed).
**.01 level of significance (two-tailed).
***.001 level of significance (two-tailed).

contact with him supplies positive rather than negative perceptions of trustworthiness. This relationship is even more surprising when compared to the effects of contact with Graham on perceptions of trustworthiness. Since Graham is a highly trusted senator, and has the reputational capital to back it up, one would expect that constituent contact would result in increased perceptions of trustworthiness. And, indeed, constituent contacts with Senator Graham enhance perceptions of trustworthiness. In this case, we might conclude that personal contact supplied unbiased information. But how about Mack? Contact with Mack, rather than unveiling evidence of a rather shoddy reputation for trustworthiness, actually enhanced perceptions of trustworthiness, and to a greater degree than with respect to Graham!

If information derived from the personal contact of voters with their legislators is shared with others, networks of extended dealings will be biased on the positive side. Such networks are unlikely to supply the type of critical assessments obtained from information pooled among consumers. Clearly, only a small proportion of the electorate avail themselves of a legislator's services, but those who do are not merely satisfied; they cannot think of anything *more* that their legislator could have done (Commission on Administrative Review 1977, 831)! Table 7.3 describes the requests made of legislators according to a 1977 national opinion survey. The nature of the requests is highly personal, such as help in obtaining social security or other types of federal benefits. Legislators excel at such tasks, and the personal treatment these requests receive impresses constituents and enhances perceptions of service. But the delivery of personalized, or to use Mayhew's (1974) term "particularized," benefits to constituents is no assurance of trustworthy behavior. For example, some interests more important to a legislator's reelection may receive greater attention, while other interests are ignored. After all, legislators distinguish among their supporters in the district, and the intensity of their loyalties (Fenno 1978, 1–30).

Constituents seem quite willing to infer the trustworthiness of their legislators, in their out-of-sight activities, from the personal attention their own individual problems receive.[9] Apparently, voters "read" their legislators' constituency services as evidence of dutiful service, and it is of course just that. But it is also little more than that. Legislators need to go beyond conscientious attention to constituent problems to warrant a reputation as a faithful agent. They need to demonstrate honesty and trustworthiness in office. I fear that legislators will be too eager to substitute service to constituents for ethical conduct if voters are too impressed with the service they receive.

The extended dealings of legislators, like businesses, should make leg-

TABLE 7.3
The Specific Nature of Requests of Congressmen, 1977[a]

Nature of Request	Percent
Wanted to get discharged from Army due to medical problems or illness in family	10
Letter written concerning legislation, public policy (e.g., gun control)	13
For information concerning Social Security, pension benefits, delayed checks	11
Seeking appointment to a military academy	4
For information, for school; request of publications	4
About a job; government work	9
Information about a relative in the service	[b]
Tax problems	2
Legal advice	1
Assistance with educational benefits under the Veteran's Administration	3
Other	44
Don't know	1
Number of cases	229

Source: Commission on Administrative Review (1977, 830).

[a]*Question*: "Have you, or has anyone in your immediate family, ever requested any kind of help or assistance from a Member of Congress or his staff?" If the respondent answered "yes," the follow-up query was posed: "What kind of help or assistance was that? What was the specific nature of the problem or request?"

[b]Less than 1 percent.

islators concerned that their reputations will suffer if they prove less than conscientious and their shirking is uncovered by a critical public. This is a major way in which reputational capital constrains cheating by businesses. Extended dealings in the market accomplish this objective by reducing the search costs of consumers through information pooling, and reducing the time span between repurchases. Both of these conditions operate to increase the costs of cheating customers. While such a network seems essential for keeping businesses honest, it is unlikely that it can function in a similar manner with respect to Congress. The personalization of most legislator–constituent contacts assures a less than critical audience. Such experiences on the part of constituents may even shape perceptions of their legislator's behavior in other areas, leading to the type of voter rationalizations that seemed to have helped check-kiting incumbents avoid electoral defeat (see chapter 6). This reduces the value of the extended dealings of legislators as constraints on unethical behavior.

REPUTATIONAL CAPITAL AND INSTITUTIONAL POWER

I have argued that premiums associated with a reputation for faithful public service deter unethical and quasi-ethical behavior. Unfortunately, these premiums may lose their force as we progress up the ladder of power in American government, thereby undermining reputational controls. There is a clear hierarchy to political power in the United States, with presidents our most powerful public officials, and senators more powerful than representatives. This hierarchy is also positively related to the likelihood of obtaining prestigious post-elective positions (if they should desire one). That is, former presidents are normally better able to find prestigious post-elective employment than senators, regardless of their levels of reputational capital. The same can be said about senators and representatives: senators are more likely to receive attractive post-elective employment than most representatives, all things being equal (appendix 6). Of course, this is *not* to say that a publicly disgraced official will obtain better post-elective employment than a trusted politician just because he or she held higher political office. The point is that, in general, reputational capital may be less important in obtaining prestigious post-elective employment as one moves up the ladder of political power in American government.

Table 7.4 shows levels of reputational capital for presidents from John Kennedy to William Clinton. Clearly, presidents are marked by low levels of reputational capital. In fact, several presidents have distinctly negative reputations (Jimmy Carter, George Bush, and William Clinton) and none of the rest can boast of even a 10 percent level of reputational capital. It is doubtful, however, that any of the living presidents would have a hard time finding a "good" job. Figures 7.1 and 7.2 show the distribution of reputational capital in the Senate and House. As expected, senators have higher levels of reputational capital than presidents, but lower than representatives. This is best seen in the fact that about 11 percent of the representatives in the study exhibited levels of reputational capital that were greater than or equal to 20 percent, but only 3 percent of the senators could boast of similar levels of reputational capital; and representatives on the whole tend to have slightly higher levels of reputational capital (mean = 9 percent) than senators (mean = 7.7 percent).

The most straightforward explanation for these institutional differences in reputational capital is that such capital is more highly valued by representatives than senators, or presidents for that matter. While senators, and certainly presidents, must endure lower levels of electoral safety than representatives, they have far less to fear from electoral de-

TABLE 7.4
Percentage of Voters Who Perceive Presidents as Faithful Agents, 1960–1992

President	Faithful Agent (%)	Unfaithful Agent (%)	Number of Cases
John Kennedy	4.4	1.0	1954
Lyndon Johnson	5.0	3.4	1834
Richard Nixon: 1960	2.9	2.5	1959
1968	6.4	6.4	3100
1972	12.8	6.6	2705
Jimmy Carter	16.4	18.0	2870
Ronald Reagan: 1980	15.0	12.6	1614
1984	10.0	7.7	2257
George Bush	6.6	8.8	2040
William Clinton	8.2	18.1	2485

Source: Compiled by author from National Election Studies, 1960–1992.

feat since they can obtain prestigious post-elective employment without high levels of goodwill. Senators, therefore, may invest less into their reputations for faithful service than representatives because they discount reputational rewards: senators can obtain prestigious post-elective employment without high levels of reputational goodwill. They (senators) may suffer by experiencing greater electoral insecurity, but the six-year term and the prospects of attractive post-elective employment make investments in a faithful-agent reputation less compelling. Consequently, reputational controls are less effective in stemming unethical behavior as one progresses up the ladder of political power.

As noted earlier (chapter 3), representatives may discount the value of reputational capital because it is unlikely that they will lose office and therefore be in a position to cash in on their reputations; moreover, the likelihood of obtaining a prestigious job is not exceedingly large anyway. And senators discount the value of reputational capital because even though it would help them get reelected, if they lose they can always find a good job without high levels of reputational goodwill. This produces a paradox: those who need reputational capital to obtain a good job are electorally safe (representatives) and therefore are unlikely to be job-hunting in the near future; and those who are less electorally secure have little need of reputational capital to obtain a good job (senators). This paradox represents another weakness in reputational controls. Not only does the influence of post-elective employment shrink as one progresses up the ladder of political power, but at the bottom rung electoral safety reduces the fear of losing election and therefore the need of a good alternative source of employment.

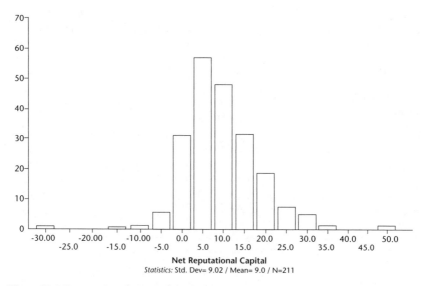

Figure 7.1 Reputational Capital in the U.S. House. *Source*: Compiled by author from National Election Studies, 1978–1994.

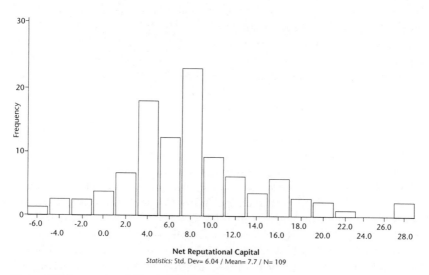

Figure 7.2 Reputational Capital in the U.S. Senate. *Source*: Compiled by author from National Election Studies, 1978–1994.

CONCLUSION

Why is the stock of reputational capital among legislators so low? There are several plausible explanations. First, institutional conditions weaken the risks of revelations of opportunism. Weak institutional penalties, imperfect policing, and high levels of electoral safety make legislators less fearful of engaging in opportunistic behavior and milking their reputations. Second, since those with low levels of reputational capital have weak incentives to forego the gains obtained through opportunistic behavior, they are likely to continue their devious behavior, and perhaps even expand their dishonesty into other areas. Opportunism continues, therefore, because the untrustworthy have few incentives to change their behavior.

Third, one of the payoffs of high levels of reputational capital is a good post-election job; however, for a variety of reasons (e.g., job competition, lack of relevant skills) even very trustworthy legislators have a difficult time obtaining prestigious post-elective employment. As a result, legislators have reason to minimize their investments in reputational capital because of the low probability that they will be able to realize the good fortune that comes from maintaining a reputation for trustworthiness. Fourth, building reputational capital requires considerable sacrifice (e.g., opportunity costs). If members are able to persevere by offering less costly alternatives as substitutes to a faithful-agent reputation, the incentives to invest in the latter will all but disappear; and voters seem all too willing to accept substitutes. Such conditions promote the milking of one's reputation.

Fifth, the paradox of reputational capital and post-elective employment may weaken the incentives for building (and investing) in a faithful-agent reputation. The least electorally safe legislators (i.e., senators) can obtain good jobs without high levels of reputational capital; hence, senators can reap a major benefit of reputational capital (i.e., attractive post-elective employment) without enduring the sacrifices associated with nurturing a faithful-agent reputation. As for the most electorally safe — House incumbents — they also face disincentives for investing heavily in their reputations as faithful agents since it is unlikely they will be seeking another career in the near future. Thus, those who could benefit the most from high levels of reputational capital in obtaining post-elective employment are safe and unlikely to need "incumbency insurance," and those more electorally marginal can obtain attractive employment without high levels of reputational capital.

Sixth, although legislators appreciate the value of prestigious post-elective employment, they are also prepared to accept substitute vocations, for example, as lobbyists. These latter positions, while admittedly lacking in prestige, may provide legislators with benefits that might offset such a loss; money might be just such a substitute, and there seems to be no lack of lucrative lobbying positions for former members of Congress. If legislators seek and are willing to accept "substitute" employment opportunities rather than prestigious ones, the benefits of reputational capital are less compelling, and the capacity of reputability to constrain opportunistic behavior all but disappears.

In sum, conditions that reduce the incentives for legislators to invest in a faithful-agent reputation promote opportunism and, unfortunately, such conditions seem to permeate Congress. We should be especially troubled by senators, since they have even fewer incentives for making large sunk investments in their reputations for trustworthiness: trust has no significant impact on their electoral vote nor their prospects for attractive post-elective employment, and perceptions of trustworthiness can be cultivated through mere contact with voters. Reputational controls seem to be at a distinct disadvantage in curtailing ethical abuse among senators.

Conclusion

THE PRECEDING ANALYSES have provided empirical evidence that some of the features of reputations that induce self-policing in the market are present to a degree in politics. There is evidence that quasi-ethical behavior (i.e., collection of honoraria) can reduce reputational capital if it should become public. In addition, there is evidence that trust is important to the electoral vote and the long-term safety of House incumbents, as well as their prospects for attractive post-elective employment if they lose office. Still, the improbable event that any damaging information will be obtained through personal contact with legislators weakens reputational controls. In the following pages I briefly summarize the arguments that underlie these empirical results.

Reputations represent more than merely "words" since voters are not interested in "words," only "actions"; so politicians have to validate their reputations to the satisfaction of constituents. "Faithful agents" do so by foregoing opportunities to exploit voter ignorance to obtain private gain; they substitute public goods for private ones. These investments function as performance bonds that bind them to high levels of ethical conduct. If the reputable politician engages in opportunistic behavior, he or she risks sacrificing these sunk investments. A reputation as a faithful agent also serves as a market signal to potential employers that the politician is conscientious, dutiful, keeps promises, and is therefore a good contractual risk. Such behavior earns a premium: it enhances electoral safety and future employment prospects.

Since other reputations are also electorally useful, some politicians develop substitutes to a faithful-agent reputation. Unfortunately, these substitute reputations do not provide the necessary performance bond to prevent opportunism from arising. Substitute reputations are also powerful cues in congressional elections and, therefore, some of the benefits of reputational capital can be obtained (electoral success) without incurring the costs of a faithful-agent reputation. Moreover, legislators can easily enhance constituent perceptions of trustworthiness through mere *personal* contact. Their personal visits to their constituencies, and the numerous services they supply, provide opportunities to engender perceptions of trust. The electoral success of legislators involved in congressional scandals, such as occurred at the House bank, combined with the electoral viability of substitutes to a faithful-agent reputation, assure that elections will be no more than highly imperfect ex post mechanisms for constraining opportunism. Premiums for trust-worthiness, and sunk investments in reputations as faithful agents, are necessary to supplement and complement the electoral imperative. Even so, these reputational incentives face their own unique set of obstacles in encouraging ethical behavior.

For one thing, senators have fewer incentives to make sizable investments in their reputations. First, trustworthiness has no significant effect on the electoral support of senators, nor does it appear to shape post-elective employment opportunities to any measurable degree (appendix 6). Second, the longer term for senators provides ample time for voters to forget the latter's transgressions. Third, personal contact with voters enhances perceptions of trust, irrespective of the incumbent's reputability (as reflected in existing levels of reputational capital). Under such conditions, we cannot expect senators to have a strong demand for reputational capital, and not surprisingly, senators on the whole exhibit low levels of such capital, especially when compared with House incumbents. Indeed, a paradox seems to arise in the relationship between the hierarchy in political offices and levels of reputational capital. Specifically, legislators who *could* benefit the most from reputational goodwill to obtain attractive post-elective employment are electorally safe and unlikely to be job-hunting in the foreseeable future — for example, U.S. Representatives — and those most electorally insecure — such as U.S. Senators and Presidents — have no need to possess high levels of reputational capital in order to obtain a good job!

Is Unethical Behavior Really that Enticing to Legislators?

An implicit assumption in this analysis is that unethical behavior is a persistent problem in Congress. Granted, ethics codes have evolved, become more stringent in their standards, and encompassed greater and greater areas of legislator behavior. Nonetheless, the more ethics laws we have, the more voters believe that legislators won't dare engage in such forbidden activities. This gives voters a false sense of security, and ignores the fact that Congress is a good place to practice opportunistic behavior. While there are many reasons for Congress to be hospitable to opportunistic legislators, three seem to be endemic to the institution: there are poor off-the-job substitutes for many congressional activities (e.g., legislative voting, foreign travel); it is futile or very costly to police the behavior of legislators; and retirement from office occurs with some frequency, thereby minimizing electoral and ethical sanctions.[1]

Legislator cheating is most likely to occur when there are poor off-the-job substitutes for congressional activities. Kalt and Zupan (1984, 283–284) make the point quite nicely:

[S]hirking by legislators may focus on nonpecuniary perquisites of office holding — although opportunities for personal pecuniary gain are certainly available. The perquisites of political office range from "fact finding" junkets and post service employment connections with rent-seeking interest groups to public notoriety, prestige, and the ability to use the power of government to impose one's own pet theories of the "good" society.

For many, if not most, congressional activities there are very few good substitutes in the private sector.

Cheating and unethical behavior also persist in Congress because it is costly if not impossible to effectively police the behavior of politicians due to problems involved in observing the latter's behavior (chapter 3). Many legislative activities are plagued by imperfect observation and moral hazard problems. Moral hazards arise because of the impossibility of observing the activities that legislators engage in, many of which are intentionally hidden from public view, like foreign junkets. Problems of imperfect observability frequently occur "when it is difficult to separate out an agent's contribution from that of random events or when an agent has private information about, say, the quality of the good being sold" (Weingast and Marshall 1988, 135). Finally, opportunism is heightened for legislators on the verge of retirement from public office. Legislators no longer facing an electorate at the end of their present term of office face incentives to cheat.[2] If elections are designed to constrain cheating and encourage faithful behavior, the absence of the electoral threat removes this constraint and encourages opportunism in the last period of officeholding.

In sum, institutional conditions assure ample enticements for opportunistic behavior on the part of rational politicians. Ethics codes are already hard pressed to mute these incentives for opportunistic behavior, and given the Supreme Court's ruling in *U.S. v. Sun-Diamond Growers of California* — that is, that prosecutors must show a direct "quid pro quo" between an official act and a gratuity — they are likely to lose more ground. Under such conditions, rational politicians should not find the costs of unethical behavior too formidable.

CAN REPUTATIONAL CAPITAL SERVE AS A "SELF-POLICING" MECHANISM?

In light of the high levels of electoral safety in Congress, can self-policing be maintained? If a reputation as a faithful agent were beneficial once one exited office, and one never knew with certainty when such an event would occur, then reputational capital could constrain opportunistic behavior. This latter condition, the uncertainty of exit through electoral defeat, seems more characteristic of Congress than we might expect, as I noted in chapter 5. Although electoral safety is relatively high, this only means that electoral defeat is rare. Unanticipated events and uncontrollable circumstances add a little uncertainty to every election; legislators always confront the possibility of defeat every time they run for reelection. Indeed, there is some evidence to suggest that the role of idiosyncratic forces, at least in senate elections, has grown over time (Kostroski 1973).

There might seem to be an inconsistency here. On the one hand I have suggested that electoral safety makes legislators less than eager to make large investments in their reputations because they can remain in office as long as they want. On the other hand, I contend that the uncertainty of reelection may encourage self-policing on the part of legislators. Both statements are correct in this sense: while electoral safety is the norm, in terms of high rates of reelection, most senators and members of Congress have experienced close encounters with electoral defeat during their legislative careers. For example, 53.3 percent of the House incumbents in the 104th Congress (1995–1996) won at least one congressional election with 55 percent or less of the vote; the comparable figure for senators is 68 percent (Ornstein et al. 1996, 68). Such experiences, although infrequent, give legislators cause to wonder about what they might be doing should the unexpected occur—namely, they lose reelection.

Electoral uncertainty also results from random terror. Unexpected events (e.g., unusually well-financed and attractive challengers) introduce a random component to election outcomes. Such elements of uncertainty encourage legislators to develop reputations that are highly marketable, and few are as economically and politically attractive as a reputation as a faithful agent. Uncertainty of this nature makes self-policing feasible. This turns attractive post-elective employment into an incentive that discourages legislators from engaging in opportunistic behavior. If legislators gain so much from a faithful-agent reputation, why don't they invest greater effort in building that reputation? Part of the problem stems from the fact that one of the benefits of a faithful-agent reputation, post-elective employment, also remains uncertain. After all, only one of three highly faithful (House) legislators obtains prestigious post-elective employment. So, while they stand to gain in terms of post-elective employment, faithful agents nonetheless face rather dim prospects.

ARE WE TOO CRITICAL OF THE ETHICAL CONDUCT OF TODAY'S POLITICIAN?

Today's Congress is far more "open" than in the past. The institution of the recorded teller vote, the opening up of committee mark-up sessions, the recording and publicizing of committee votes, the enactment of financial and campaign disclosure laws, the televising of congressional proceedings, and the like, have increased the availability of information about legislators. But does this necessarily imply greater ethical conduct? John Ferejohn (1999) contends that legislator-agents have incentives to reveal information about themselves to encourage their constituents to entrust them with greater societal resources and wealth, rather than to demonstrate ethical fidelity.

While there seems to be a lot less overt bribery, this does not mean that corruption has not taken other less conspicuous forms. Corruption may now find more unobtrusive venues, making it far more difficult to detect. As long as politics in general, and legislatures in particular, are marked by costly monitoring, poor off-the-job substitutes for certain office activities, and last-period problems, unethical behavior and opportunism will always be a problem. Enterprising legislators can always exploit areas where ethics codes are ambiguous or silent.

Explicit rules have made it only difficult, but not impossible, to escape detection for unethical conduct. In fact, we might expect legislators to invest greater resources in avoiding detection. That is, the greater openness of congressional practices and procedures may have made detection of unethical behavior less difficult, but this may only prompt legislators interested in concealing their unethical behavior to invest greater resources in avoiding detection. And there are, of course, ample ways for legislators to make detection of their activities more costly or impossible to police. The efforts by Congress to make it more difficult for individuals or groups *outside of Congress* to instigate ethics charges against legislators can be viewed as just one such way to avoid ethics challenges (Congressional Quarterly 1997, 2199–2200). Thus, greater openness may not have had the desired effect of constraining cheating. Unethical conduct may find less detectable outlets, and legislators may expand and intensify their efforts to avoid policing.

In raising the bar for ethical conduct, have we assured that our legislators will fall far short of accepted standards? While there is some truth in such an argument, the counterarguments are equally persuasive. First, ethics codes have evolved *in response to the unethical conduct* of legislators. Ethics codes may be stronger today than in the past, but it is unlikely that our legislators fall short of these standards because they have been set too high. Ethics codes were strengthened because many legislators were engaging in questionable ethical practices; ethics codes only changed to stem breakdowns in the ethical conduct of legislators. Second, political scandals awaken voters to the possibilities and opportunities awaiting politicians interested in private gain rather than public service; ergo, voters place greater importance on trustworthiness and honesty, and rational legislators would be wise to do the same. Thus, legislators who follow ethical standards, or exceed them, are well-rewarded. As I demonstrated with respect to the publicizing of legislator honoraria, legislators can take advantage of lapses in the judgments of their colleagues, through public revelations of congressional misdeeds or scandals, to build reputational capital. The ability of legislators to point with pride to the absence of ethics violations or charges against them, enhances their reputational capital. Only the dishonest and untrustworthy will view the standards as being too lofty. Third, ethics codes, as noted, are only *minimal* standards; it is unlikely that such standards are excessive. And it is hard to conceive of a rational legislature as designing standards of conduct that less than a majority of its members could easily satisfy! Thus, higher ethical standards seem an unlikely cause of the low levels of reputational capital among legislators.

In sum, the argument that low levels of reputational capital are a consequence of the public (or legislators themselves) raising ethical standards higher and higher, is problematic. The public is relatively uninformed about such matters, and those most informed—legislators—have reason to favor the least rigorous standards possible. Higher ethical standards are not the reason that our legislators look so bad in terms of their reputations for trustworthiness. They do that to themselves.

CAN REPUTATIONAL CONTROLS BE STRENGTHENED?

Can anything be done to strengthen the capacity of reputational controls to curb legislator opportunism? In the case of senators and presidents, the solution seems all too obvious: employers need to place a greater emphasis on a politician's reputation for trustworthiness in their hiring practices. If they (employers) were to do so, exiting senators and presidents could no longer count on their previous positions of power and visibility to pave the way to attractive post-elective employment. Reputational capital would then take on added importance, especially given the electoral vulnerability of senators. With respect to congressmen and -women, the solution is just the opposite: Representatives need to be able to secure attractive post-elective employment at a greater rate. This would restore, or enhance, the importance of the premium paid faithful agents. Indeed, one external benefit of better private sector employment after elective office would be to improve the quality of the candidate pool, thereby attracting individuals prepared to make the necessary reputational investments that constrain unethical conduct. The findings presented here suggest that unfortunately only a few of the most trusted and conscientious representatives obtain prestigious post-elective employment.

But why should the employment prospects for the truly faithful be so dim? It is impossible to answer this question with the data presently available; however, several explanations seem plausible. First, political skills are not easily translated into valuable economic resources or explicit factors of production, except in the case of lobbying. No matter how large an office staff a representative oversees, or the breadth of policy issues deliberated, management positions in corporations present unique challenges. Second, corporations' managers and major stockholders may harbor deep suspicions about the values and work habits of politicians. This makes them reticent about employing politicians, especially in prestigious positions where stockholders and managers have a difficult time monitoring the behavior of employee-politicians. Third, politicians may be merely the unfortunate victims of the economic marketplace: employment in prestigious positions is highly competitive (e.g., more competent and experienced employees than jobs). Finally, since most legislators are able to hold on to their congressional seats for about six terms (Erikson 1976), they may be too old to obtain important managerial positions when they finally do leave office.

George Stigler (1972, 96) once contended that it always pays to give customers and voters what they want. If he's correct, voters have the incentives for promoting contractual adherence in their own hands: voters' refusal to accept "substitutes" for faithful agents will encourage politicians to build reputational capital and, in the process, reduce the attraction of opportunism. Voters seem all too willing, all too often, to accept substitutes for faithful agents. So, too, with employers. The reluctance of employers to hire politicians for reasons aside from their good "name" would encourage politicians to keep their reputations unspoiled.

Too often we query legislators by asking them their plans upon retirement or why they have chosen to retire. A more informative question would be to ask what they would do if they lost their next reelection; then their expectations would reveal the extent to which they intended to invest heavily in their reputations, or milk them. A faithful agent, anticipating a payoff for foregoing years of private gain, would expect a prestigious job. The least faithful, after years of milking their reputations, could only anticipate less prestigious jobs, though no doubt, highly paying ones (e.g., lobbying government). Sunk investments in a faithful-agent reputation constrain unethical behavior, but the trick is how to entice rational legislators to make these investments rather than seek less costly alternatives — substitute reputations and less prestigious post-elective employment. In the absence of adequate incentives, low

TABLE C.1
Average News Interest by Subject Category (Top Individual Items in Each
Category Shown)

	Average Extent News Stories Are Followed (%)			
News Topic	Very Closely	Fairly Closely	Not too Closely	Not at all Closely
Natural Disaster (15 stories)[a]	45	35	13	7
San Francisco earthquake (73%, Nov. 1989)				
Hurricane Andrew (66%, Sept. 1992)				
Floods in the Midwest (65%, Aug. 1993)				
Man-Made Disaster (16 stories)	44	34	15	7
Challenger disaster (80%, July 1986)				
Crash of TWA Flight 800 (69%, July 1996)				
Little girl in well in Texas (69%, Oct. 1987)				
Military/Terrorism—U.S. (43 stories)	41	35	16	8
End of Persian Gulf War (67%, March 1991)				
Iraq's invasion of Kuwait (66%, Aug. 1990)				
Iraq's occupation of Kuwait (63%, Oct. 1990)				
Court Rulings (9 stories)	30	33	21	15
Supreme Court ruling/flag burning (51%, July 1989)				
Supreme Court ruling/abortion (47%, July 1989)				
Supreme Court ruling/ PA abortion law (28%, May 1992)				
Economy/Business (52 stories)	30	33	20	16
Increase in price of gas (62%, Oct. 1990)				
Reports on U.S. economy (49%, March 1993)				
Stock Market Crash (40%, Oct. 1987)				

TABLE C.1 *Continued*

	Average Extent News Stories Are Followed (%)			
News Topic	Very Closely	Fairly Closely	Not too Closely	Not at all Closely
Crime (29 stories) O. J. Simpson case (48%, June 1994) Attack on Nancy Kerrigan (45%, Jan. 1994) Arrest of Unabomber suspect (44%, April 1996)	27	32	22	18
Social Issues (25 stories) Rodney King case/verdict and riot (70%, May 1992) Videotaped beating of Rodney King (46%, March 1991) Gays in the military/lifting ban (45%, March 1993)	26	32	22	20
Domestic Policy (67 stories) Clinton's economic plan (49%, March 1993) Clinton's health care plan (49%, Sept. 1993) Bush Administration/U.S. drug crisis (40%, Sept. 1989)	25	33	22	19
Physical/Science (13 stories) Cold weather in the Northeast (51%, Jan. 1994) Flight of space shuttle (50%, Oct. 1988) Hot weather/greenhouse effect (42%, Aug. 1988)	25	31	22	21
Sports (15 stories) Summer Olympics in Atlanta (45%, July 1996) Winter Olympics (33%, Feb. 1992) World Series (31%, Oct. 1988)	24	25	20	30
Campaigns and Elections (37 stories) Outcome of presidential election (55%, Dec. 1996)	23	34	24	19

TABLE C.1 *Continued*

News Topic	Average Extent News Stories Are Followed (%)			
	Very Closely	Fairly Closely	Not too Closely	Not at all Closely
News about President campaign (43%, Oct. 1988) Presidential election campaign (42%, Sept. 1992)				
National Politics (35 stories) Federal government shutdown (42%, Jan. 1996) Bush's heart problems (38%, May 1991) Oliver North's sentencing (37%, July 1989)	21	30	24	24
International Policy (83 stories) Opening of Berlin Wall (50%, Nov. 1989) Political upheaval in China (47%, July 1989) Breakup of Soviet Union (47%, Oct. 1991)	20	32	25	22
Political Scandal (31 stories) Congressional check bouncing scandal (36%, April 1992) Arrest of DC Mayor Barry (28%, Feb. 1990) Gary Hart withdrawal/Donna Rice (28%, Sept. 1987)	17	29	27	26
Celebrity Scandal (16 stories) Jim Bakker guilty verdict (33%, Oct. 1989) Mike Tyson's rape trial (32%, Feb. 1992) Banishment of Pete Rose (30%, Sept. 1989)	16	26	27	30
Military/Terrorism–Non-US (49 stories) Failed coup in Panama (29%, Oct. 1989)	14	31	29	25

TABLE C.1 *Continued*

	Average Extent News Stories Are Followed (%)			
News Topic	Very Closely	Fairly Closely	Not too Closely	Not at all Closely
Revolution in Romania (28%, Jan. 1990)				
Gas attack in Tokyo subway (26%, March 1995)				
Personality/Entertainment (16 stories)	14	22	25	38
Nixon's death and funeral (36%, May 1994)				
Networks and television violence (26%, Aug. 1993)				
Roseanne Barr singing national anthem (21%, Aug. 1990)				

Source: Parker and Deane (1997).
ᵃTop three news stories are listed in each category.

levels of reputational capital will mark Congress, and most members will seek only the minimum required standards of ethical conduct. And the problem is complicated by the unpleasant reality that voters don't really care that much about ethical violations. Table C.1 describes voter interest in various news stories. Less than one in five respondents on average followed news stories about political scandals "very closely."

There are, of course, incentives for legislators to make significant investments in their reputations for faithful conduct. Although the adequacy of the premium paid trustworthy politicians may be open to debate, being reputable is more than its own reward.[3] There is evidence that it enhances the career longevity of House incumbents as long as their trustworthiness is not too excessive, and it is more important than basic legislator characteristics in promoting attractive post-elective employment, if reelection fails. Reputational capital, however, seems less useful to senators since it has neither a significant effect on their electoral votes nor prospects for attractive post-elective employment. Reputational controls, like elections and ethics codes, have their limits.

The question that prompted this inquiry was whether reputational controls, or incentives, were effective constraints on unethical conduct in Congress. There appears to be evidence supportive of that conclusion, but some unsettling caveats remain. While there is no reason to be sanguine about this state of affairs, clear incentives exist to promote reputational controls on unethical and opportunistic behavior — primarily, the loss of sunk investments in one's reputation, and the premiums that are awarded faithful politicians in terms of electoral safety and attractive post-elective employment. Self-policing may not be the panacea for the ethical control of elected officials, but there are properties of reputations that should give us hope that such a mechanism can induce propriety on the part of even self-interested politicians.

Most Important Characteristic for Legislator to Possess: Examples of Category Content

Trust
 Honesty
 Integrity
 Fair
 Represents the people
 Trustworthy

Service
 In touch with people
 Works for people
 Good listener
 Helpful
 Good relationship with people in district
 Stand by people who elected them

Performance
 Knowledge
 Effective in running their office
 Experience
 Credibility

Personal Characteristics
 Outgoing
 Open-minded
 Good speaking ability
 Caring
 Charisma
 No personal problems
 Patriotism
 Nonpartisanship
 Someone from local neighborhood
 Interest in politics
 Pride
 Not racist
 Friendly
 Independent
 Well-rounded

Able to stand up for himself or herself
Ambition
Objectivity
Sense of humor
Good reputation
Intelligence
Compassion
Balanced view

Issues
Democrat
Republican
Willing to help minorities
Conservative
Awareness of issues
Values education
Spends less money
Aware of environment

Examples of Categories of Employment

Prestigious Government
   Appointment on Illinois International Post District Board
   Secretary of Human Resources (North Carolina)
   Commission on Defense Base Closing and Realignment
   Secretary, Department of Environment, Health and Natural Resources (North
      Carolina)
   U.S. Attorney for North District of Alabama
   Environmental Protection Agency Administrator — Middle Atlantic
   Associate Judge for U.S. Court of Veterans' Appeals
   Secretary of Transportation (Washington, D.C.)

Prestigious Private
   Named Chair in Center for Strategic and International Studies
   Visiting Professor
   Fellow at Harvard University's John F. Kennedy School of Government
   Professor at Stanford University Law School
   President of School of Theology at Claremont College (California)
   Lecturer at John F. Kennedy School of Government
   Named Professor

Business
   Board of directors of several multinational corporations and New York Stock
      Exchange
   Member of various corporate boards
   Owner and Chief Executive Officer at Heftel Broadcasting
   Chairman and CEO, American Stock Exchange
   Chairman, Research Development Board of Carolinas Medical Center
   Chairman and President of CliniCorp Northeast Division
   Chairman, Eagle Newspapers (twenty newspapers in three states)

Codes for Identifying Faithful Agents

National Election Study "Candidate Code" Numbers	Like or Dislike Referencing an Attribute of a Faithful Agent
0213	Dependable/trustworthy/reliable; a man you can trust with the responsibilities of government ("trust" in the capability sense, rather than the honesty sense)
0214	Undependable/untrustworthy/unreliable; a man you can't trust with the responsibilities of government
0217	His record in public service; how well he's performed in previous offices
0224	Has fulfilled/kept (campaign) promises
0225	Has not fulfilled/kept (campaign) promises
0307	People have confidence in him
0308	People don't have confidence in him
0319	Careful/cautious/good judgment
0320	(Too) impulsive/careless/bad/poor judgment
0323	Represents (well) the views of the district
0324	Does not represent (well) the views of the district
0401	Honest/sincere; keeps promises; man of integrity; means what he says; not tricky; open/candid; straightforward; fair
0402	Dishonest/insincere; breaks promises; no integrity; doesn't mean what he says; tricky; not open/candid; not straightforward
0403	Man of high principles/ideals; high moral purposes; idealistic
0404	Lacks principles/ideals
0407	Public servant; man of duty; conscientious; hard-working; good attendance record in Congress; dedicated
0408	Does not take public service seriously; lazy; poor attendance record in office; not dedicated
0409	Doesn't use office for personal benefit; not in office to maximize personal benefit
0410	Uses/in office (mostly) for personal benefits (junket trips, big salary, other perks)
0431	Unsafe/unstable; dictatorial; craves power; ruthless
0502	Controlled by party regulars/bosses, machine

National Election Study "Candidate Code" Numbers	Like or Dislike Referencing an Attribute of a Faithful Agent
0503	Not controlled by party regulars/bosses
0832	Selfish, only help themselves
0835	Has a well-defined set of beliefs, definite philosophy; does not compromise on principles; has a (clear) understanding of goals he stands for
0836	Has poorly defined set of beliefs; lacks a definite philosophy; compromises on principles; has no clear understanding of goals he stands for

Source: National Election Studies, 1978–1994, note 7 ("Party and Candidate Codes").

Lifetime Judicial Appointments: 1965–1996[a]

	%	N	President		%	N	President
1965	10.5	14	Johnson	1981	23.2	45	Reagan
1966	45.9	61		1982	23.7	46	
1967	25.6	34		1983	21.1	41	
1968	18.0	24		1984	32.0	62	
1969	16.9	33	Nixon	1985	34.9	83	Reagan
1970	32.8	64		1986	21.0	50	
1971	35.9	70		1987	31.1	74	
1972	14.4	28		1988	13.0	31	
1973	17.6	21	Nixon	1989	10.9	24	Bush
1974	31.9	38		1990	22.6	50	
1975	16.8	20	Ford	1991	36.7	81	
1976	33.6	40		1992	29.9	66	
1977	11.6	32	Carter	1993	18.1	37	Clinton
1978	11.2	31		1994	36.8	75	
1979	55.4	153		1995	36.3	74	
1980	21.7	60		1996	8.9	18	

Source: *The Weekly Compilation of Presidential Documents*, Office of the Federal Register, National Archives and Records Administration, Washington, D.C., 1965–1996, vols. 1–31.

[a]The data include the nominations made by the president for federal judgeships which carry life tenure. These courts are also called Article III courts because their power comes directly from the U.S. Constitution. The courts are the District Courts, Circuit Courts of Appeal, and the U.S. Supreme Court. Also included and carrying life tenure is the U.S. Court of International Trade.

Examples of Prestigious Post-Elective Employment Positions

Chair of the U.S. Merit Systems Protection Board
U.S. Attorney for Northern District of Alabama
Emeritus Professor, San Diego University
Member, California Public Utilities Commission
Member, Supreme Court Judicial Nominating Commission, State of Colorado; member, Colorado Water Conservation Board
Chair, Federal Housing Finance Board
Senior Vice President, Ringling Bros. and Barnum and Bailey Circus
Professor of Government, Jacksonville University
Director, Tobacco and Peanuts Division, U.S. Department of Agriculture
Fellow, John F. Kennedy School of Government; member, board of directors, Commodity Credit Corporation; Under Secretary for Rural Economic and Community Development, Department of Agriculture
Visiting Professor, University of Louisville School of Law
Ambassador to Trinidad and Tobago
President, NAACP
Deputy Director, U.S. Arms Control and Disarmament Agency
Ambassador to Canada
President, Z. Smith Reynolds Foundation
Ambassador to Panama
Secretary of Housing and Urban Development; vice presidential nominee
Counselor to the President, World Bank
Member, International Joint Commission, United States and Canada
Chair and Chief Executive Officer, American Stock Exchange; Ambassador to Mexico
Chair, Campaign for America Project; Chair, National Bankruptcy Review Commission
Deputy Secretary of Revenue, Commonwealth of Pennsylvania
Member, Federal Mine Safety and Health Review Commission
President, United Negro College Fund; Special Advisor on Haitian Affairs to President and Secretary of State
Member, Board of Regents, University of Texas
Board Member, Advanced Technology Laboratories and Discovery Institute

Electoral Defeat and Post-Elective Employment for Senators in the Analysis

Senator Who Lost Election	Net Reputational Capital	Year of Defeat	Post-Elective Employment
Lowell Weicker	− 4.7	1988	Visiting Professor, George Washington University; and Governor of Connecticut in 1990
John Melcher	− 3.3	1988	a
Rudy Boschwitz	3.6	1990	Candidate for U.S. Senate in 1996
Robert Kasten	− .1	1992	a
Wyche Fowler	1.3	1992	Ambassador to Saudi Arabia
Alan Dixon	3.5	1992	Chair, Defense Base Closure and Realignment Commission
Terry Sanford	5.1	1992	a
Harris Wofford	− 2.3	1994	Chief Executive Officer of the Corporation for National and Community Service
Jim Sasser	7.1	1994	Ambassador to China

Source: Biographical Directory of the American Congress, 1774–1996. Congressional Quarterly, 1997.

^aNo information available.

Notes

INTRODUCTION

1. I am reminded of Nobel Laureate George Stigler's admonition to economists more than thirty years ago in his important article, "The Theory of Economic Regulation." After bemoaning the monopolistic effects of regulations, such as licenses to practice a trade, he concludes the article by encouraging economists to "quickly establish the license to practice on the rational theory of political behavior" (Stigler 1971, 18). Economists appear to have heeded Stigler's warning by applying their trade to a whole range of political topics, ranging from elections to legislatures. With respect to the study of political corruption and excesses, they appear to have cornered the market, so to speak, insofar as these topics are considered a central avenue of disciplinary interest. So, to rephrase Stigler, political scientists need to muscle-in on the economists' monopolistic control over the analysis of these topics or we will surely lose any claim to studying these important political phenomena.

CHAPTER 1
WHAT IS OPPORTUNISM AND HOW DO WE CONTROL IT?

1. For instance, former Representative Mary Rose Oakar (D-Ohio) wrote 213 checks at the now-defunct House bank. She also pleaded guilty in September 1997 to charges of conspiracy and violation of campaign finance laws — two federal misdemeanor charges. Apparently, she fabricated contributor names to disguise the sources of political donations.
2. John Peters and Susan Welch suggest that corrupt political acts can be described in terms of the "public official" involved, the "favor" provided, the "payoff gained," and the "recipient" of the preferential treatment. They contend that "probably the most corrupt situation is when the donor is the public official himself. If the public official can directly enrich himself by tapping the public till, he himself is the donor. Examples of this include padding the expense account, using public funds for personal travel, using money allocated for office expenses for personal activities, and so on" (Peters and Welch 1978, 977). The acts of opportunism discussed and analyzed in this chapter can be described in terms of these conceptual distinctions. In every instance, the acts of opportunism are done as part of an official's duties, and the legislator is the recipient of his or her own opportunism; the legislator obtains a private short-range benefit that is specific in nature (e.g., leisure) and unrelated to campaign contributions. Legislators, in short, are able to ingratiate themselves through opportunistic actions, as well as ostensibly corrupt ones.
3. It might be argued that political parties could serve as mechanisms to con-

trol opportunism by punishing members who behave unethically. While parties do, to some extent, police the conduct of their members through internal partisan organizations and procedures, they generally lack the necessary leverage. Indeed, political parties have a difficult time even getting their members to follow the party line:

> If partisan pressure is to attenuate individual legislator ties to constituency, then there must be some mechanism of leverage on individual legislators by which the party enforces its positions. Control over party nominations and committee assignments in the United States, for example, are the tools with which party leaders could impose greater observance of party positions. . . . Essentially the same conclusion is reached if we examine other possible sources of party leverage over individual legislators. . . . It should come as no surprise that, if anything, parties facilitate the ties to constituency by giving legislators district-relevant committee assignments, by not intruding in local nominating processes, and by distributing campaign and institutional resources in a relatively evenhanded fashion. (Shepsle and Weingast 1984, 432)

CHAPTER 2
HOW REPUTATIONS CONTROL CHEATING

1. Klein et al. (1978, 306) make the correspondence between the premiums earned by businesses and their reputations in this way:

> These fixed (sunk) costs of supplying credibility of future performance are repaid or covered by future sales on which a premium is earned. In equilibrium, the premium stream is then merely a normal rate of return of the "reputation," or "brand name" capital created by the firm by these initial expenditures.

2. The survey question was worded in the following way: "Now let me read you some actions some people have taken about changing things they didn't like about government — things like corruption in government, unjust laws, or failure to get public services. For each action taken, tell me if you would certainly do that, possibly do it, possibly not do it, or certainly not do it." Responses of "certainly do that," or "possibly do it," are collapsed into the same category to arrive at the figures reported. The percentages reported here are from Committee on Government Operations (1973, 259).

3. Aside from spreading reputational information, there is another way in which the extended dealings of businesses may reduce opportunism on the part of the latter. One factor that reduces cheating on product quality is a shorter period for the repurchase of a product (Klein and Leffler 1981, 624). A business, given a shorter period for the detection of product-cheating and its punishment through subsequent lost sales, has less incentives to cheat its customers. Extended dealings, "by making it more likely that the individuals one is sharing product-quality information with (e.g., family and friends) have purchased from the same firm, lowers the potential short-run cheating gain by essentially reducing the repurchase period" (Klein and Leffler 1981, 619).

4. In 1994, the expenditures in House campaigns totaled $347,375,296 and 282 candidates spent over $500,000 on their campaigns. The figures on the Senate are quite similar: $279,826,576 was spent (in total) on Senate campaigns in 1994, and the mean was $3,997,523. In the 104th Congress (1995–96) the mean term was 4.8 for House incumbents. In 1994, 387 House incumbents sought reelection, while 48 retired. For a more detailed description of the historical treads in these data, see Ornstein et al. (1996).

5. A background in politics may be important to the running of large corporations. See Agrawal and Knoeber (2001, especially pp. 179–180).

Chapter 3
Problems in the Market for Legislators

1. It might be argued that although a reputation for trustworthiness is valuable, it is difficult to validate because there are just too few opportunities to demonstrate one's honesty. I disagree. As Richard Fenno (1978, 58) has observed, "expressions conveying a sense of their [legislators'] honesty flicker through their statements concerning financial disclosure, limitations on campaign contributions, refusals to go on junkets, return of office allowances to the treasury, appointment of citizen watchdog committees to oversee campaign finances, etc." It is doubtful that it is the lack of opportunity that prevents legislators from accumulating reputational capital.

Chapter 4
Hypotheses, Measurement, and Data

1. William Bianco (1994) offers an alternative to the conceptualization of trust used in this study. While trust is interpreted here as integrity and honesty for the most part, Bianco suggests that it be defined in terms of leeway, specifically, voting leeway. Voting leeway, according to Bianco, enables legislators to behave as "trustees," voting their own judgments rather than the less-informed opinions of constituents, without fear of electoral reprisal. It is possible, but highly doubtful, that "leeway" could be used by legislators to avoid voter anger over public revelations of their unethical or corrupt activity. Bianco's conceptualization of trust as leeway seems more relevant in discussing voting behavior rather than acts of opportunism. Indeed, if leeway encouraged legislators to exploit moral hazards, there would be a positive relationship between trust — that is, reputational capital — and acts of opportunism. As will be evident, there is no empirical evidence of such a relationship: high levels of reputational capital are associated with less opportunism, not more.

2. "Goodwill" is defined here in the same manner as in Stigler (1961, 218): "continued patronage by consumers without continued search (that is, no more than occasional verification)."

3. Such small samples in some districts might give the reader cause to worry that the measurements are biased, resulting in a noticeable skewness in the dis-

tribution of reputational capital among House incumbents. However, as figure 7.1 shows, the distribution in reputational capital among House incumbents fits quite well a normal distribution (i.e., symmetry around the mean).

4. One major advantage to this analysis is that measurement of reputational capital could be obtained prior to major instances of congressional opportunism such as revelations of honoraria income and check kiting. In retrospect, no better period for examining opportunism and trustworthiness in Congress could be expected. Unfortunately, the data for senators do not permit the calculation of reputational capital prior to acts of opportunism (e.g., public revelations of honoraria income); hence, I depend less upon the senate data for testing the theory because of potential measurement contamination.

5. The size of the sample surveys were 989 respondents in the 1988 survey and 1,083 respondents in the 1997 survey; the 1999 survey contained 676 respondents.

6. The survey question is worded in the following way: "If you had a problem that Representative (name of incumbent) could do something about, do you think (he/she) would be very helpful, somewhat helpful, or not very helpful to you?"

CHAPTER 5
CONSTRAINING OPPORTUNISM

1. Influence-buying cases are enormously difficult to prove because the actions are rarely documented on paper and are normally based far more on personal relationships. For example, Representative Shuster (R-Pa.) may have had a role to play in corruption and influence-peddling surrounding Boston's $10 billion "Big Dig," the most expensive public works project in U.S. history. This project (The Central Artery Project) to sink Boston's main elevated highway underground has resulted in costly and litigious situations where the state sought to take privately held land. Shuster, who at the time was the senior Republican on the subcommittee that controlled highway construction, didn't raise a dime from Massachusetts in the 1988 election, but during the next two years, 10 percent of his individual contributions came from the state, with nearly all of it from individuals involved with land-taking disputes with the state. This is not really too surprising since Shuster raises considerable campaign money out of the state, especially in areas with pending highway projects or proposals (e.g., Texas, Illinois); his contribution reports are like a map to roads that don't yet exist, but could someday.

2. Lott (1987, 170) suggests that ideological reputations serve to constrain last-period problems:

> While nonideological politicians face a last-period problem, ideological ones do not necessarily face one. The cost of ideologues not voting for their constituency in the last period is foregone utility. If a politician's ideological preferences correspond *exactly* to the wishes of his constituents, the politician's voting pattern should continue to reflect these interests even when the cost of shirking in terms of foregone future votes is low.

Lott finds no evidence that ideological "shirking" or "cheating" occurs among retiring legislators, but he finds that the latter do vote less ("participatory shirking") in the last period.

3. Lame-duck legislators are defined as members leaving to pursue another office, through either appointment or election, or just plain retiring. In all instances, legislators are probably aware they are in their last period. If untrustworthy legislators, anticipating a run for another office, are reticent about junketing before their next election, they would be behaving like faithful agents— those with higher levels of reputational capital. The result would be that the "untrustworthy" and the "trustworthy" would display similar levels of foreign travel in their last period of officeholding. Such conditions would work against the hypothesized relationship, attenuating rather than maximizing any observed relationship.

4. Rostenkowski was indicted and charged with embezzling hundreds of thousands of dollars in public funds ($668,000) and using tens of thousands of dollars in campaign funds ($52,267) for personal purposes between mid-1971 and late 1992. In a plea agreement, Rostenkowski also admitted sending payroll checks through the mail to pay employees who performed personal political services, and using public funds to buy gifts in the House stationery store for friends.

5. Measurements of the reputational capital of retiring representatives are taken *prior* to their last term of office. Exiting legislators are defined as those who retired, sought another office, or accepted appointment to another position outside of Congress; excluded are representatives who lost their reelection bids or died while in office.

CHAPTER 6
REPUTATIONAL CAPITAL AND JOB SECURITY; OR, IF TRUSTWORTHY LEGISLATORS ARE AT A PREMIUM ARE THEY PAID ONE?

1. The ANES surveys are made available by the Inter-University Consortium for Political and Social Research. Data used here were collected in 1988 and 1990 (see the Senate Elections in Context 1988–1990 Pooled File, ICPSR study no. 9580); the 1988 universe included all individuals of voting age before or on November 8, 1988, and residing in a house with a telephone in the fifty states, and the 1990 universe contained all persons of voting age on or before November 6, 1990, and otherwise conforming to the strictures for 1988.

2. Question wording: "We are interested in how people are getting along financially these days. Would you say that you (and your family living here) are better off or worse off financially than you were a year ago?"

3. For the congressional surveys used here, respondents were asked their feelings about the Democratic and Republican incumbent candidates for both House and Senate seats.

4. Respondents were asked the following questions: "If you had a problem that your Representative could do something about, do you think he/she would be very helpful, somewhat helpful, or not very helpful to you"; and "how good

a job would you say Representative/Senator . . . does of keeping in touch with the people in your district/state — does he/she do a very good, fairly good, fairly poor, or poor job of keeping in touch with the people in this district/state?"

5. The question reads as follows: "Now we would like your opinion about the way Senator/Representative . . . has voted on bills that have come up in the U.S. Senate/House of Representatives in Washington. Would you say that you have generally agreed with the way he/she has voted on bills, agreed and disagreed about equally, generally disagreed, or haven't paid much attention to this?"

6. Each of these variables is constructed in the same manner: number of likes mentioned concerning a particular incumbent attribute minus number of dislikes mentioned concerning that same attribute. For example, the number of dislikes voiced by a respondent about his or her incumbent's constituency attentiveness is subtracted from the number of likes mentioned by the same individual about attentiveness. See Parker (1989) for a discussion and description of the items used to measure constituent trust, and Parker and Parker (1993) for an analysis of the dimensionality of the trust items, as well as their relationship to personal contact with one's representative. Some of the assessments used in Table 4.1 include trust (honest, sincere, doesn't use office for personal benefit, has kept campaign promises), experience (experienced, inexperienced, not qualified for the job), personal characteristics (intelligent, safe, likable, democratic), constituency (keeps people well informed, helps people, has helped the district or state economy), domestic policy positions (relating to such policy areas as government economic controls, welfare and poverty problems, Social Security and pensions, unemployment compensations, and aid to education), and foreign policy positions (relating to such policy areas as foreign aid, strong vs. weak military position, Russia, Eastern Europe, and Latin America). Also note that the variable "year" has been coded 1 if 1990, 0 otherwise.

7. The actual estimate of the electoral costs of corruption remains an issue of contention. Peters and Welch, for example, concluded that incumbents suffered a loss of between 6 and 11 percent of the expected vote; later, Welch and Hibbing, in extending the time frame of the Peters-Welch analysis another 12 years, concluded that the vote loss was about 9 percent (Welch and Hibbing 1997, 234).

8. Gary Jacobson and Michael Dimock (1994) disagree with Groseclose and Krehbiel (1994) about the effects of overdrafts on retirements, reporting a highly significant relationship between overdrafts and retirements (608, table 3). Richard Hall and Robert Van Houweling (1995) found that the probability of retirement for a legislator who kited fifty checks was virtually indistinguishable from a House member who kited no checks.

9. The question was: "Representatives who wrote only a few bad checks should not be voted out of office, but Representatives who wrote a lot of bad checks should be voted out of office."

10. The question was: "Writing a bad check is not a serious enough mistake to disqualify someone for office."

11. There is also no evidence that the abuse of congressional prerogatives

reduces the vote significantly for the accused candidates (Peters and Welch 1980, 705, table 3).

12. If voters realized that the flow of federal dollars to their constituencies was influenced more by district demand and long-established formulae, rather than the actual occupant of the congressional seat, they might be less impressed by the largess of incumbents (see, for example, Ray 1980).

13. There are some measurements of the actual vote loss that resulted from the check-kiting scandal at the House bank, but unfortunately no consensus. I estimated that kiting one hundred or more checks cost an incumbent about 6 percent of the vote (Parker 1996, 150); Dimmock and Jacobson (1995, 1157) concluded that involvement in the scandal reduced the reported vote for incumbents by about 5 percent; Alford et al. (1994) found no relationship whatsoever.

CHAPTER 7
WEAKNESSES IN REPUTATIONAL CONTROLS

1. There is an interesting controversy in public choice regarding whether politicians are "search" or "experience" goods. This distinction arises from Phillip Nelson's (1970, 1974) work that seeks to differentiate goods according to whether the quality of the product can be determined at the time of purchase: the quality of "search goods" (e.g., clothing) can be assessed, for the most part, prepurchase while the quality of "experience goods" — as the term implies — can be evaluated only after purchase (e.g., automobiles). This distinction has been applied to politicians' reputations to explain the ideological behavior of legislators (Lott 1987; Dougan and Munger 1989). That is, the argument is made that ideological reputations serve as market signals as to how legislators will behave in Washington once elected. In contrast, others contend (Crain and Goff 1986) that advertising one's brand name is a strategy reserved for politicians behaving as experience goods. While an important controversy in its own right, it remains a digression from the major point of this analysis in this sense: whether or not politicians are actually search or experience goods, previous career accomplishments seem to have little effect in enhancing a faithful-agent reputation.

2. Question: "There are many ways in which public officials such as senators can have contact with Floridians. Please tell me if you have had contact with or learned anything about either of Florida's senators in the following ways: met (Bob Graham, Connie Mack); spoke to (Bob Graham, Connie Mack); talked to a member of his (Bob Graham, Connie Mack) staff; know someone who has had contact with (Bob Graham, Connie Mack)."

3. The lack of trust in Connie Mack is also evident in the fact that 43.8 percent of the 1,083 repsondents positioned on the scale gave no positive — that is, trusting — responses, as compared to 30.7 percent for Graham and 34 percent for Clinton. The variances, however, are quite similar: Graham (2.105), Mack (2.048), and Clinton (1.939).

4. Questions: "Thinking now of state government in Tallahassee. How much of the time do you think you can trust Florida State government to do what is

right—just about always, most of the time, or only some of the time?" "How much of the time do you think you can trust the government in Washington, D.C. to do what is right—just about always, most of the time, or only some of the time?" Each question is coded so that the least trusting response—"only some of the time"—receives the lowest value.

5. Question: "Now think about the taxes you pay. From your personal standpoint, please tell me for each tax I read off to you if you feel it is too high, too low, or about right—Florida state sales tax, local property tax, state gasoline tax?" Each item is coded so that the response indicating the greatest burden—"too high"—receives the lowest value.

6. Questions: "We are interested in how people are getting along financially these days. Would you say that you (and your family) are better off or worse off financially than you were a year ago?" "Now looking ahead, do you think that a year from now you (and your family) will be better off financially or worse off or about the same?" Each item is coded so that the least favorable economic prediction—"worse off financially"—receives the lowest value.

7. In the 1988 survey, respondents were queried about the following issues. "Should the government in Washington see to it that every person has a good job and a good standard of living? Or should the government just let each person get ahead on his own? Or do you feel you are in the middle between these two positions?" "Should the government in Washington make every effort to improve the social and economic positions of blacks and other minority groups? Or should the government make no special effort to help minorities because they can help themselves? Or do you feel you are in the middle between these two positions?" "Should the taxes people pay to the national government be reduced even if public services have to be cut? Or do we need these public services even if it means paying the same taxes? Or do you feel you are in the middle between these two positions?" "Some people feel that defense spending should be decreased. Do you think that defense spending should be increased, decreased, or do you feel that defense spending should be kept at the same level?" A respondent's preference for Democratic party positions is represented by responses supportive of guaranteed incomes and employment ("government should provide jobs"), improve conditions for Blacks and other minorities ("government should make an effort to provide special help"), maintain services rather than reduce taxes ("maintain services"), and decrease defense spending. Each preference favoring a traditional Democratic Party position receives a 1, with a respondent's total score reflecting the sum of his or her support of Democratic Party policies.

8. In the 1997 survey, Floridians were asked which party they felt was closer to their own positions on the following issues. "Democratic policy including issues such as social programs, minimum wages, and unemployment. Defense policy including issues such as the defense budget, weapons systems, and military bases. Economic policy including issues such as reducing the deficit, taxes, and setting budget priorities. Moral issues, such as abortion, school prayer, and policies dealing with the family. On state issues. On national issues?" A respondent received a 1 for each response that indicated a closer proximity to the perceived position of the Democratic Party; an individual's total score is the sum

of the individual's issue proximity to the Democratic Party over this range of issues.

9. In earlier research (Parker 1989, 187), I found that the perceived attentiveness of House incumbents toward their districts increased the latter's reputational capital (i.e., mentions of elements of a faithful-agent reputation in open-ended likes/dislikes questions like those used here).

CONCLUSION

1. Between 1986 and 1994, nearly forty representatives and six senators retired each Congress (Ornstein et al. 1996, 60–61).

2. For example, John Lott (1987) found no evidence that legislators facing retirement altered their ideological voting patterns — in other words no shirking in the last period; however, he also reported that retiring House members voted less frequently. The latter behavior seems quite symptomatic of shirking in the last period.

3. For a thought-provoking study of factors producing reputational capital for large U.S. firms, see Fombrun and Shanley (1990).

References

Agrawal, Anup, and Charles R. Knoeber. 2001. "Do Some Outside Directors Play a Political Role?" *Journal of Law and Economics* 64:179–198.

Akerlof, George H. 1970. "The Market for 'Lemons': Quality Uncertainty and the Market Mechanism." *Quarterly Journal of Economics* 74:488–500.

Alchian, Armen A., and Harold Demsetz. 1972. "Production, Information Costs, and Economic Organization." *American Economic Review* 62:777–795.

Alford, John, Holly Teeters, Daniel S. Ward, and Rick Wilson. 1994. "Overdraft: The Political Cost of Congressional Malfeasance." *Journal of Politics* 56:788–801.

Allen, Franklin. 1984. "Reputation and Product Quality." *Rand Journal of Economics* 15:311–327.

Barro, Robert J. 1973. "The Control of Politicians: An Economic Model." *Public Choice* 14:19–42.

Beard, Edmund, and Stephen Horn. 1975. *Congressional Ethics*. Washington, D.C.: Brookings Institution.

Beatty, R. P., and J. R. Ritter. 1986. "Investment Banking, Reputation, and Underpricing of Initial Public Offerings." *Journal of Financial Economics* 15:213–232.

Becker, Gary S. 1968. "Crime and Punishment: An Economic Approach." *Journal of Political Economy* 76:169–217.

Becker, Gary S., and George J. Stigler. 1974. "Law Enforcement, Malfeasance, and the Compensation of Enforcers." *Journal of Legal Studies* 3:1–18.

Bianco, William T. 1994. *Trust*. Ann Arbor: University of Michigan Press.

Born, Richard. 1990. "The Shared Fortunes of Congress and Congressmen: Members May Run from Congress, but They Can't Hide." *Journal of Politics* 52:1223–1241.

Buchanan, James M., and Gordon Tullock. 1962. *The Calculus of Consent*. Ann Arbor: University of Michigan Press.

Cain, Bruce, John Ferejohn, and Morris Fiorina. 1987. *The Personal Vote*. Cambridge, Mass.: Harvard University Press.

Carmines, Edward G., and Richard A. Zeller. 1979. *Reliability and Validity Assessment*. Beverly Hills: Sage Publications.

Coase, Ronald H. 1960. "The Problem of Social Cost." *Journal of Law and Economics* 3:1–44.

Coase, Ronald H. 1937. "The Nature of the Firm." *Economica* 4:386–405.

Commission on Administrative Review, U.S. House of Representatives. 1977. *Final Report*, 95th Congress, 1st session, H. Doc. 95–272.

Committee on Government Operations, U.S. Senate. 1973. *Confidence and Concern: Citizens View American Government*, 93rd Congress, 1st Session.

Congressional Ethics. 1992. Washington, D.C.: Congressional Quarterly Press.

Congressional Quarterly. 1997. *Biographical Directory of the American Congress, 1774–1996*. Alexandria, Va.: Congressional Quarterly Staff Directories.

Congressional Quarterly Weekly Report. 1997. "Filing Complaints in House: Now for Members Only?" September 20, 1997: 2199–2200.

Cook, Thomas D., and Donald T. Campbell. 1979. *Quasi-Experimentation*. Boston: Houghton Mifflin.

Cox, Gary W., and Mathew D. McCubbins. 1993. *Legislative Leviathan*. Berkeley: University of California Press.

Crain, W. Mark, and Brian Goff. 1986. "Televising Legislatures: An Economic Analysis." *Journal of Law and Economics* 29:405–421.

Crain, W. Mark, Donald R. Leavens, and Robert D. Tollison. 1986. "Final Voting in Legislatures." *American Economic Review* 76:833–841.

Davis, Michael L., and Michael Ferrantino. 1996. "Towards a Positive Theory of Political Rhetoric: Why Do Politicians Lie?" *Public Choice* 88:1–13.

DeAlessi, Louis, and Robert J. Staaf. 1994. "What Does Reputation Really Assure? The Relationship of Trademarks to Expectations and Legal Remedies." *Economic Inquiry* 32:477–485.

Dimock, Michael, and Gary C. Jacobson. 1995. "Checks and Choices: The House Bank Scandal's Impact on Voters in 1992." *Journal of Politics* 57:1143–1159.

Dougan, William R., and Michael C. Munger. 1989. "The Rationality of Ideology." *Journal of Law and Economics* 32:119–142.

Downs, Anthony. 1957. *An Economic Theory of Democracy*. New York: Harper and Row.

Erikson, Robert S. 1990. "Economic Conditions and the Congressional Vote: A Review of the Macrolevel Evidence." *American Journal of Political Science* 34:373–399.

Erikson, Robert S. 1976. "Is There Such a Thing as a Safe Seat?" *Polity* 9:623–632.

Fama, Eugene F. 1980. "Agency Problems and the Theory of the Firm." *Journal of Political Economy* 88:288–307.

Fama, Eugene F., and Michael C. Jensen. 1983. "Agency Problems and Residual Claims." *Journal of Law and Economics* 26:327–349.

Fearon, James D. 1999. "Electoral Accountability and the Control of Politicians: Selecting Good Types versus Sanctioning Poor Performance." In *Democracy, Accountability, and Representation*, edited by Adam Przeworski, Susan C. Stokes, and Bernard Manin, 55–97. Cambridge: Cambridge University Press.

Fenno, Richard F., Jr. 1996. *Senators on the Campaign Trail*. Norman: University of Oklahoma Press.

Fenno, Richard F., Jr. 1982. *The United States Senate: A Bicameral Perspective*. Washington, D.C.: American Enterprise Institute.

Fenno, Richard F., Jr. 1978. *Home Style*. Boston: Little, Brown.

Fenno, Richard F., Jr. 1973. *Congressmen in Committees*. Boston: Little, Brown.

Ferejohn, John. 1999. "Accountability and Authority: Toward a Theory of Political Accountability." In *Democracy, Accountability, and Representation*, edited by Adam Przeworski, Susan C. Stokes, and Bernard Manin, 131–153. Cambridge: Cambridge University Press.

Ferejohn, John. 1986. "Incumbent Performance and Electoral Control." *Public Choice* 50:5–25.

Figlio, David W. 2000. "Political Shirking, Opponent Quality, and Electoral Support." *Public Choice* 103:271–284.

Fiorina, Morris P. 1978. "Economic Retrospective Voting in American National Elections: A Micro Analysis." *American Journal of Political Science* 22:426–443.

Fiorina, Morris P. 1977. *Congress: Keystone of the Washington Establishment.* New Haven, Conn.: Yale University Press.

Fiorina, Morris P., and Roger Noll. 1979. "Majority Rule Models and Legislative Elections." *Journal of Politics* 41:1081–1104.

Fombrun, Charles, and Mark Shanley. 1990. "What's in a Name? Reputation Building and Corporate Strategy." *Academy of Management Journal* 33:233–258.

Fowler, Linda L., and Robert D. McClure. 1989. *Political Ambition: Who Decides to Run for Congress.* New Haven, Conn.: Yale University Press.

Frey, Bruno S. 1993. "Does Monitoring Increase Work Effort? The Rivalry with Trust and Loyalty." *Economic Inquiry* 31:663–670.

Goldenberg, Edie N., and Michael W. Traugott. 1984. *Campaigning for Congress.* Washington, D.C.: Congressional Quarterly Press.

Groseclose, Timothy, and Keith Krehbiel. 1994. "Golden Parachutes, Rubber Checks, and Strategic Retirements from the 102nd House." *American Journal of Political Science* 38:75–99.

Hall, Richard L., and Robert Van Houweling. 1995. "Avarice and Ambition: Representatives' Decisions to Run or Retire from the U.S. House." *American Political Science Review* 89:121–136.

Hays, William L. 1973. *Statistics for the Social Sciences.* New York: Holt, Rinehart and Winston.

Heal, Geoffrey. 1976. "Do Bad Products Drive Out Good?" *Quarterly Journal of Economics* 95:499–502.

Hinich, Melvin J., and Michael C. Munger. 1996. *Ideology and the Theory of Political Choice.* Ann Arbor: University of Michigan Press.

Holmström, Bengt. 1978. "Moral Hazard and Observability." *Bell Journal of Economics* 10:74–91.

Ippolito, Pauline M. 1990. "Bonding and Nonbonding Signals of Product Quality." *Journal of Business* 63:41–60.

Jacobson, Gary C. 1990a. "Does the Economy Matter in Midterm Elections?" *American Journal of Political Science* 34:400–404.

Jacobson, Gary C. 1990b. *The Electoral Origins of Divided Government.* Boulder, Colo.: Westview Press.

Jacobson, Gary C. 1987. *The Politics of Congressional Elections*, 2d ed. Boston: Little, Brown.

Jacobson, Gary C., and Michael Dimock. 1994. "Checking Out: The Effects of Bank Overdrafts on the 1992 House Elections." *American Journal of Political Science* 38:601–624.

Jarrell, Gregg, and Sam Peltzman. 1985. "The Impact of Product Recalls on the Wealth of Sellers." *Journal of Political Economy* 93:512–536.

Jensen, Michael C., and William H. Meckling. 1976. "Theory of the Firm: Managerial Behavior, Agency Costs, and Ownership Structure." *Journal of Financial Economics* 3:305–360.

Johannes, John R., and John C. McAdams. 1981. "The Congressional Incumbency Effect: Is It Casework, Policy Compatibility, or Something Else? An Examination of the 1978 Election." *American Journal of Political Science* 25:512–542.

Kalt, Joseph P., and Mark A. Zupan. 1990. "The Apparent Ideological Behavior of Legislatures: Testing for Principal-Agent Slack in Political Institutions." *Journal of Law and Economics* 33:103–131.

Kalt, Joseph P., and Mark A. Zupan. 1984. "Capture and Ideology in the Economic Theory of Politics." *American Economic Review* 74:279–300.

Karpoff, Jonathan M., and John R. Lott. 1993. "The Reputational Penalty Firms Bear from Committing Criminal Fraud." *Journal of Law and Economics* 36:757–802.

Kau, James B., and Paul H. Rubin. 1979. "Self-Interest, Ideology, and Logrolling in Congressional Voting." *Journal of Law and Economics* 22:365–384.

Klein, Benjamin, Robert G. Crawford, and Armen A. Alchian. 1978. "Vertical Integration, Appropriable Rents, and the Competitive Contracting Process." *Journal of Law and Economics* 21:297–326.

Klein, Benjamin, and Keith B. Leffler. 1981. "The Role of Market Forces in Assuring Contractual Performance." *Journal of Political Economy* 89:615–641.

Klein, Daniel B., ed. 1997. *Reputation.* Ann Arbor: University of Michigan Press.

Klein, Daniel B. 1997. "Trust for Hire: Voluntary Remedies for Quality and Safety." In *Reputation*, edited by Daniel B. Klein, 97–133. Ann Arbor: University of Michigan Press.

Korin, Basil P. 1975. *Statistical Concepts for the Social Sciences.* Cambridge: Winthrop Publishers.

Kostroski, Warren E. 1973. "Party and Incumbency in Post War Senate Elections: Trends, Patterns, and Models." *American Political Science Review* 67:1213–1234.

Kotowitz, Yehuda, and Frank Mathewson. 1979. "Advertising, Consumer Information, and Product Quality." *Bell Journal of Economics* 10:566–588.

Kramer, Gerald H. 1971. "Short-Term Fluctuations in U.S. Voting Behavior, 1896–1964." *American Political Science Review* 65:131–143.

Krasno, Jonathan S. 1994. *Challengers, Competition, and Reelection.* New Haven, Conn.: Yale University Press.

Kreps, David M., and Robert Wilson. 1982. "Reputation and Imperfect Information." *Journal of Economic Theory* 27:253–279.

Laband, David N., and Bernard F. Lentz. 1985. "Favorite Sons: Intergenerational Wealth Transfers Among Politicians." *Economic Inquiry* 23:395–414.

Landes, William M., and Richard A. Posner. 1975. "The Independent Judiciary in an Interest-Group Perspective." *Journal of Law and Economics* 18:875–901.

Larson, Stephanie Greco. 1990. "Information and Learning in a Congressional District: A Social Experiment." *American Journal of Political Science* 34:1102–1118.

Leland, Hayne E. 1979. "Quacks, Lemons, and Licensing: A Theory of Minimum Quality Standards." *Journal of Political Economy* 87:1328–1346.

Lipsey, R. G., and Kelvin Lancaster. 1955. "The General Theory of Second Best." *Review of Economic Studies* 23:11–32.

Lott, John R. 1990. "Attendance Rates, Political Shirking, and the Effect of Post-Elective Office Employment." *Economic Inquiry* 28:133–150.

Lott, John R., Jr. 1987. "Political Cheating." *Public Choice* 52:169–186.

Lott, John R., Jr. 1986. "Brand Names and Barriers to Entry in Political Markets." *Public Choice* 51:87–92.

Lott, John R., and Michael Davis. 1992. "A Critical Review and an Extension of the Political Shirking Literature." *Public Choice* 74:461–484.

Lott, John R., and Robert W. Reed. 1989. "Shirking and Sorting in a Political Market with Finite-lived Politicians." *Public Choice* 61:75–96.

Mann, Thomas E. 1978. *Unsafe at Any Margin*. Washington, D.C.: American Enterprise Institute for Public Policy Research.

Markus, Gregory B. 1979. *Analyzing Panel Data*. Beverly Hills: Sage Publications.

Mayhew, David R. 1974. *Congress: The Electoral Connection*. New Haven, Conn.: Yale University Press.

McChesney, Fred S. 1987. "Rent Extraction and Rent Creation in the Economic Theory of Regulation." *Journal of Legal Studies* 16:101–118.

McCurley, Carl, and Jeffery J. Mondak. 1995. "Inspected by #1184063113: The Influence of Incumbents' Competence and Integrity in U.S. House Elections." *American Journal of Political Science* 39:864–885.

Merry, Sally Engle. 1997. "Rethinking Gossip and Scandal." In *Reputation*, edited by Daniel B. Klein, 47–74. Ann Arbor: University of Michigan Press.

Milgrom, P., and J. Roberts. 1986. "Relying on the Information of Interested Parties." *Rand Journal of Economics* 17:18–32.

Miller, Ross M., and Charles R. Plott. 1985. "Product Quality Signaling in Experimental Markets." *Econometrica* 53:837–872.

Miller, Warren E., Donald R. Kinder, and Steven J. Rosenstone. 1993. *American National Election Study, 1992: Pre- and Post-Election Survey*. Center for Political Studies, Ann Arbor, University of Michigan.

Mitchell, Mark L. 1989. "The Impact of External Parties on Brand-Name Capital: The 1982 Tylenol Poisonings and Subsequent Cases." *Economic Inquiry* 27:601–618.

Mitchell, Mark L., and Michael Maloney. 1989. "Crisis in the Cockpit? The Role of Market Forces in Promoting Air Travel Safety." *Journal of Law and Economics* 32:329–355.

Moe, Terry M. 1984. "The New Economics of Organization." *American Journal of Political Science* 28:739–777.

Mondak, Jeffery J. 1995. "Competence, Integrity, and the Electoral Success of Congressional Incumbents." *Journal of Politics* 57:1043–1069.

National Archives and Records Administration. 1965–1996. *The Weekly Compilation of Presidential Documents*, vols. 1–31. Washington, D.C.: Office of the Federal Register.

Nelson, Douglas, and Eugene Silberberg. 1987. "Ideology and Legislator Shirking." *Economic Inquiry* 25:15–25.

Nelson, Phillip. 1976. "Political Information." *Journal of Law and Economics* 19:315–336.

Nelson, Phillip. 1974. "Advertising as Information." *Journal of Political Economy* 82:729–754.

Nelson, Phillip. 1970. "Information and Consumer Behavior." *Journal of Political Economy* 78:311–329.

Niskanan, William A. 1971. *Bureaucracy and Representative Government*. Chicago: Rand McNally.

Nye, J. S. 1967. "Corruption and Political Development: A Cost-Benefit Analysis." *American Political Science Review* 61:417–427.

Olson, Mancur. 1965. *The Logic of Collective Action*. Cambridge, Mass.: Harvard University Press.

Ornstein, Norman J., Thomas E. Mann, and Michael J. Malbin. 1996. *Vital Statistics on Congress 1995–1996*. Washington, D.C.: American Enterprise Institute.

Parker, Glenn R. 1996. *Congress and the Rent-Seeking Society*. Ann Arbor: University of Michigan Press.

Parker, Glenn R. 1992. *Institutional Change, Discretion, and the Making of Modern Congress: An Economic Interpretation*. Ann Arbor: University of Michigan Press.

Parker, Glenn R. 1989. "The Role of Constituent Trust in Congressional Elections." *Public Opinion Quarterly* 53:175–196.

Parker, Glenn R. 1986. *Homeward Bound: Explaining Changes in Congressional Behavior*. Pittsburgh: University of Pittsburgh Press.

Parker, Glenn R. 1981. "Incumbent Popularity and Electoral Success." In *Congressional Elections*, edited by Joseph Cooper and L. Sandy Maisel, 249–279. Beverly Hills: Sage Publications.

Parker, Glenn R., and Roger H. Davidson. 1979. "Why Do Americans Love Their Congressmen So Much More Than Their Congress?" *Legislative Studies Quarterly* 4:53–61.

Parker, Glenn R., and Suzanne Parker. 1998a. "The Economic Organization of Legislatures and How It Affects Congressional Voting." *Public Choice* 60: 117–129.

Parker, Glenn R., and Suzanne Parker. 1998b. "Public Trust in Political Leaders." Paper prepared for presentation at the Hendricks Symposium on "Public Dissatisfaction with Government," University of Nebraska, Lincoln. October 8–11, 1998.

Parker, Glenn R., and Stephen Powers. 2002. "Searching for Symptoms of Political Shirking: Congressional Foreign Travel." *Public Choice* 110:173–191.

Parker, Suzanne, and Glenn R. Parker. 1993. "Why Do We Trust Our Congressman?" *Journal of Politics* 55:442–453.

Parker, Kimberly, and Claudia Deane. 1997. "Ten Years of the PEW News Interest Index." The Pew Research Center for The People and the Press. February 28, 2000 <*http://www.people-press.org/aapor.htm*>.

Peltzman, Sam. 1984. "Constituent Interest and Congressional Voting." *Journal of Law and Economics* 27:181–210.

Peters, John G., and Susan Welch. 1980. "The Effects of Charges of Corruption on Voting Behavior in Congressional Elections." *American Political Science Review* 74:697–708.

Peters, John G., and Susan Welch. 1978. "Political Corruption in America: A Search for Definitions and a Theory." *American Political Science Review* 72:974–984.

Polsby, Nelson W. 1968. "The Institutionalization of the U.S. House of Representatives." *American Political Science Review* 62:144–168.

Ragsdale, Lynn. 1996. *Vital Statistics on the Presidency*. Washington, D.C.: Congressional Quarterly.

Ray, Bruce. 1980. "Federal Spending and the Selection of Committee Assignments in the U.S. House of Representatives." *American Journal of Political Science* 23:494–510.

Rogow, Arnold A., and Harold Lasswell. 1963. *Power, Corruption and Rectitude*. Englewood Cliffs, N.J.: Prentice-Hall.

Romero, David W. 1996. "The Case of the Missing Reciprocal Influence: Incumbent Reputation and the Vote." *Journal of Politics* 58:1198–1207.

Rose-Ackerman, Susan. 1999. *Corruption and Government*. New York: Cambridge University Press.

Rubin, Paul H., R. Dennis Murphy, and Gregg Jarrell. 1988. "Risky Products, Risky Stocks." *Regulation* 12:35–39.

Rundquist, Barry S., Gerald S. Strom, and John C. Peters. 1977. "Corrupt Politicians and Their Electoral Support: Some Experimental Observations." *American Political Science Review* 71:954–963.

Saloma, John S., III. 1969. *Congress and the New Politics*. Boston: Little, Brown.

Schmalensee, Richard. 1978. "A Model of Advertising and Product Quality." *Journal of Political Economy* 86:485–503.

Sears, David O., and Jack Citrin. 1985. *Tax Revolt: Something for Nothing in California*. Cambridge, Mass.: Harvard University Press.

Shapiro, Carl. 1983. "Premiums for High Quality Products as Returns to Reputations." *Quarterly Journal of Economics* 98:659–679.

Shepsle, Kenneth A., and Barry R. Weingast. 1987. "The Institutional Foundations of Committee Power." *American Political Science Review* 81:85–104.

Shepsle, Kenneth A., and Barry R. Weingast. 1984. "Political Solutions to Market Problems." *American Political Science Review* 78:417–434.

Shepsle, Kenneth A., and Barry R. Weingast. 1981. "Structure-induced Equilibrium and Legislative Choice." *Public Choice* 37: 503–519.

Smith, Adam. 1997. "Lecture on the Influence of Commerce on Manners." In

Reputation, edited by Daniel B. Klein, 17–20. Ann Arbor: University of Michigan Press.

Spence, Michael. 1973. "Job Market Signaling." *Quarterly Journal of Economics* 77:355–374.

Stigler, George J. 1972. "Economic Competition and Political Competition." *Public Choice* 13:91–106.

Stigler, George J. 1971. "The Theory of Economic Regulation." *Bell Journal of Economics and Management Science* 2:137–146.

Stigler, George J. 1962. "Information in the Labor Market." *Journal of Political Economy* 70:49–73.

Stigler, George J. 1961. "The Economics of Information." *Journal of Political Economy* 69:213–225.

Stokes, Donald E., and Warren E. Miller. 1962. "Party Government and the Saliency of Congress." *Public Opinion Quarterly* 26:531–546.

Telser, Lester G. 1980. "A Theory of Self-Enforcing Agreements." *Journal of Business* 22:27–44.

Telser, Lester G. 1964. "Advertising and Competition." *Journal of Political Economy* 72:537–562.

Tuckman, Bruce W. 1972. *Conducting Educational Research*. New York: Harcourt, Brace, Jovanovich.

Tufte, Edward R. 1978. *Political Control of the Economy*. Princeton, N.J.: Princeton University Press.

Tullock, Gordon. 1981. "Why So Much Stability?" *Public Choice* 37:189–202.

Vanbeek, James R. 1991. "Does the Decision to Retire Increase the Amount of Political Shirking?" *Public Finance Quarterly* 19:444–456.

Wattenberg, Martin P. 1998. *The Decline of American Political Parties, 1952–1996*. Cambridge, Mass.: Harvard University Press.

Weingast, Barry R. 1988. "The Congressional-Bureaucratic System: A Principal Agent Perspective (with applications to the SEC)." *Public Choice* 44:147–191.

Weingast, Barry R., and William J. Marshall. 1988. "The Industrial Organization of Congress; or, Why Legislatures, Like Firms, Are Not Organized as Markets." *Journal of Political Economy* 96:132–163.

Welch, Susan, and John R. Hibbing. 1997. "The Effects of Charges of Corruption on Voting Behavior in Congressional Elections, 1982–1990." *Journal of Politics* 59:226–239.

Williamson, Oliver E. 1981. "The Modern Corporation: Origins, Evolution, Attributes." *Journal of Economic Literature* 19:1537–1568.

Williamson, Oliver E. 1975. *Markets and Hierarchies: Analysis and Antitrust Implications*. New York: Free Press.

Wright, Gerald C., Jr., and Michael B. Berkman. 1986. "Candidates and Policy in United States Senate Elections." *American Political Science Review* 80:567–588.

Yiannakis, Diana Evans. 1982. "House Members' Communication Styles: Newsletters and Press Releases." *Journal of Politics* 43:1049–1071.

Zupan, Mark A. 1990. "The Last-Period Problem in Politics: Do Congressional Representatives Not Subject to a Reelection Constraint Alter Their Voting Behavior?" *Public Choice* 65:167–180.

Name Index

Subject Index

adverse selection, 12, 21–22
assumptions: extended dealings, 9, 42–46; gossip, 42–43; implications for legislators, 50–51; information pooling, 43; information shortcuts, 9, 40–42; job security, 10–11, 48–50; post-elective employment, 48–50; premiums for honesty, 10–11, 47–50; rationality, 9, 39–40; sunk investments, 9, 46–47, 51. *See also* economic models of the firm, similarities between firms and politicians; opportunism, reputational controls on; post-elective employment; price premium; reputation; reputational capital

cheating: in economics and politics, 2; reasons for cheating in Congress, 140–141. *See also* reputational control
citizen contact: businesses and politicians, 43–46, 59; measurement of, 127; as sources of information, 56–59, 132. *See also* economic models of the firm; legislator-constituent contact; reputational capital, effects of extended dealings
congressional casework, 59, 132. *See also* reputational capital, effects of extended dealings; reputational control, and personal experience
congressional foreign travel, 16–17, 25, 91–93, 97–98. *See also* opportunism, congressional junkets
corruption, 159n.2, 164n.7. *See also* cheating; opportunism

economic models of the firm: business mythology, 37; differences between firms and politicians, 8, 48, 53–54, 59, 132–133; and reputational control, 6, 9–11, 13; similarities between firms and politicians, 2, 10–11, 13, 45–47, 54; voters and consumers compared, 2, 40, 43, 45–46, 125–126, 133
elections: control of politicians, 7, 18, 26–27, 115–122; House and Senate, 106–111

electoral motive. *See* assumptions, premiums for honesty; elections, control of politicians
ethics codes: effectiveness, 27, 29–31, 142–144; informal enforcement, 29–31; penalties, 27–29; problems in, 3–4; voter interest, 146–149. *See also* opportunism; reputational control, problems with controlling legislators
extended dealings, 9, 42–46, 58–59, 127–133, 160n.3

faithful-agent reputation: coding, 154–155; substitutes for, 62–67, 106–109, 139

home style, 57–58, 108. *See also* perceived trustworthiness, effects of personal contact; reputation; reputational control, and informational bias
honoraria, 17–18, 92–93, 95, 99–101. *See also* opportunism
hypotheses, 72–74, 99, 103, 124

incomplete contracts, 23

last-period problems: in Congress, 25, 91–92, 162n.2; in economics and politics, 23, 25, 97–98; in judicial appointments, 87–88; lifetime judicial appointments, 1965–1996, 156
legislator-constituent contact, 46, 57–59, 73, 130–133. *See also* citizen contact; perceived trustworthiness; reputational capital; reputational control
"lemons" problem, 21–22. *See also* adverse selection

monitoring: and congressional hearings, 88–89, problems, 4–5, 60–62. *See also* moral hazards
moral hazards, 22–23, 91, 141

opportunism: check kiting, 26, 93–94; congressional junkets, 25; defined, 15–16, 24, 85; economic solutions to, 31–